Early Childhood Play **Matters**

Intentional teaching through play: birth to six years

Shona Bass
and
Kathy Walker, OAM

Acknowledgments

We would like to thank Sally Ward for her wonderful support and guidance during the photo shoot and for her considered contributions to the text that reflect her passion for, and expertise in, early childhood education.

We appreciate and acknowledge the contribution from the following centres for making their engaging, intentional and creative learning environments available during the photo shoot: Wattletree Early Childhood Centre, Wilson St Kindergarten and St Kilda & Balaclava Kindergarten.

We also thank and acknowledge Simone Pedder and Janelle Thorne (Anula Primary School) for their feedback on sections of the book; and other early childhood educators across Australia who have worked with us during the development of the Walker Learning pedagogy.

Published in 2025 by Amba Press, Melbourne, Australia
www.ambapress.com.au

First published in 2015 by ACER Press, an imprint of
Australian Council for Educational Research Ltd

© 2025 Shona Bass and Kathy Walker

Photographs with thanks to Wattletree Early Childhood Centre, St Kilda & Balaclava Kindergarten, and Wilson Street Kindergarten.

This book is copyright. All rights reserved. Except under the conditions described in the Copyright Act 1968 of Australia and subsequent amendments, and any exceptions permitted under the current statutory licence scheme administered by Copyright Agency Limited (www.copyright.com.au), no part of this publication may be reproduced, stored in a retrieval system, transmitted, broadcast or communicated in any form or by any means, optical, digital, electronic, mechanical, photocopying, recording or otherwise, without the written permission of the publisher.

Edited by Anne Mulvaney
Cover design by JAC Design
Indexed by Julie King

ISBN: 9781923569041 (pbk)
ISBN: 9781923569058 (ebk)

A catalogue record for this book is available from the National Library of Australia.

Contents

Preface ... iv

Chapter 1 Reclaiming and reframing early childhood education ... 1
Introduction ... 2
Developing an educational philosophy ... 2
Developmentally appropriate practice (DAP) ... 7
Summary ... 13

Chapter 2 Intentional teaching: it's everything and all we do, all of the time ... 15
Introduction ... 16
What does intention mean in relation to education in early childhood? ... 16
Developing intentional teaching in early childhood ... 17
Fact check: busting the myths ... 20
Summary ... 21

Chapter 3 Neuroscience informing evidence-based practice ... 23
Introduction ... 24
Nature and nurture: not all children are born equal ... 24
Brain development: 100 billion neurons and building ... 25
Executive function skills: skills for success in life ... 25
The power of social and emotional skills ... 28
Brain development: uniqueness and diversity ... 30
Importance of open-ended play experiences ... 30
Contextual experience and then repeat, repeat ... and repeat! ... 31
Relationships, relationships, relationships: face time ... 32
Summary ... 35

Chapter 4 Communication and relationships with children, colleagues and parents ... 37
Introduction ... 38
Emotional intelligence model of building relationships ... 38
Proactive strategies to guide children's behaviour and build relationships ... 44
A child not engaged? ... 48
A centre philosophy and strategies ... 49
Working proactively with colleagues and parents ... 49
Summary ... 51

Chapter 5 Overview of play from a teaching and learning perspective ... 53
Introduction ... 54
Play-based pedagogy ... 54
Types of play ... 55
Stages of play ... 56
Some key characteristics of play ... 57
Summary ... 59

Chapter 6 Creating an intentional and engaging learning environment ... 61
Introduction ... 62
Key learning experiences ... 62
Key features of an engaging and intentional learning environment ... 69
Summary ... 74

Chapter 7 Planning, documentation and assessment: want your life back? ... 75
Introduction ... 76
Back to basics and fundamentals ... 76
Planning and documentation ... 78
Other tools, templates and processes ... 89
Summary ... 91

Chapter 8 Walker Learning: early childhood education (babies to preschool) ... 93
Introduction ... 94
Walker Learning: key elements (early childhood to Year 8) ... 95
Walker Learning: key pedagogical practice across early childhood to Year 8 ... 96
Walker Learning: key pedagogical practice in early childhood ... 99
Implementation of Walker Learning: babies to preschool ... 101
Summary ... 103

Bibliography ... 104
Index ... 106

Preface

Early Childhood Play Matters brings us to where Walker Learning and play-based learning really begins. Developing a solid basis and foundation of learning for children in their early years requires planned, proactive and intentional play-based learning. It requires an environment that is rich with provocations for children to investigate and explore, and educators who explicitly extend, support and scaffold children in the learning, development and acquisition of skills.

A high standard of teaching and learning in the early childhood years is reflected by a pedagogy:

- that embraces cultural relevance, family and environmental contexts
- that provides open-ended play-based learning that is planned and scaffolded by adults
- where educators are mindful and reflective in their practice
- where educators are self-aware and articulate
- where educators are expert in their body of knowledge and communication about children.

Walker Learning provides systems and practices that hold together teams of early childhood educators in a consistent approach that ensures continuity and predictability for children, educators and families.

This book provides chapters on a range of key elements of practice, including how to minimise time on planning and documentation so that records are clinical and professional but not time-consuming; how to set up play learning experiences to promote skills (not merely reacting to the interests of children); how to scaffold with intention and purpose for learning; how to communicate effectively, to grow in professionalism and self-awareness as an educator; and how to honour and build relationships with children and families.

Play Matters: Investigative learning for preschool to Grade 2 and *Engagement Matters: Personalised learning for Grades 3 to 6* provide the continuation of play- and project-based learning and how to personalise and engage children as they move throughout their education and schooling.

Early Childhood Play Matters sets the pace and the culture of where it all begins – building upon the relationships, interactions and learning that have been started between parents and children at home.

Chapter 1: Reclaiming and reframing early childhood education

This chapter describes the key aims of this book, which are to:

- empower early childhood educators to renew themselves in professionalism, their body of knowledge and evidence-based practice
- provide practical support for documentation, learning play areas, relationship building and clarity around our key purposes in early childhood education
- provide opportunities for reflection on practice
- provide a model for play-based learning that is developmentally and culturally appropriate.

This book has been written especially for early childhood educators working with children from birth to six years of age in kindergartens, preschool and childcare settings. Chapter 1 is the foundation that the subsequent chapters build upon.

Chapter 2: Intentional teaching: it's everything and all we do, all of the time

The starting point of all planning for early childhood education (or in fact for a child of any age) is to consider:

- Where is this child at developmentally and in their learning?

- What is next or where to next for this child?
- How do I engage this child in a learning experience that is open-ended and focused on skill acquisition and process (not outcome)?

In this chapter we examine each of these components of intentional teaching and guide the educator towards rigorous and authentic intentional teaching.

Chapter 3: Neuroscience informing evidence-based practice

Understanding some critical elements of developmental neuroscience and psychology is critical to inform pedagogical practice, which helps to provide developmentally appropriate practice and sets each child up for success. In this chapter we provide a synopsis of aspects of brain development and how these inform practice. This chapter provides the evidence base for any rigorous early childhood pedagogy.

Chapter 4: Communication and relationships with children, colleagues and parents

In this chapter we present an introduction to an emotional intelligence model to facilitate relationships and communication with children. Walker Learning embeds emotional intelligence throughout the pedagogy. Becoming more emotionally intelligent is a lifelong journey and this chapter presents the very beginning of this journey.

Chapter 5: Overview of play from a teaching and learning perspective

Play in itself is worth a whole book and is an entire discipline, so this chapter is designed to give a brief review of the theories of play and play pedagogy, and key elements of play as a pedagogy, rather than provide the overarching details of the discipline of okay play.

Chapter 6: Creating an intentional and engaging learning environment

The learning environment is described in some education theories as the 'third teacher' and is a critical component of a high-quality early childhood education. The aim of an intentional and engaging learning environment is to promote a sense of wonder, exploration, investigation and interest in a rich range of materials, resources and opportunities in which the child can engage. Creating this type of environment requires expertise, knowledge and skill. This chapter shows the educator the why and the how – the colour section at the end of this chapter is a real highlight!

Chapter 7: Planning, documentation and assessment: want your life back?

This chapter guides early childhood educators back to the basics of educating, back to the core business of the profession and back to the basics of why and how to effectively plan and document. It clarifies the purpose of planning and documentation and presents Walker Learning planning and documenting tools that provide accountability and, more importantly, personalising learning for the children.

Chapter 8: Walker Learning: early childhood education (babies to preschool)

This chapter summarises key elements presented in previous chapters and outlines how they look in practice throughout a day or week. This chapter also describes the terminology used in Walker Learning so there is greater consistency across all educators, families and children. This provides greater security and predictability in the children's lives.

Chapter 1
Reclaiming and reframing early childhood education

'Play is the highest form of research.'

Albert Einstein

Introduction

This book has been written especially for early childhood educators working with children from birth to six years of age in kindergartens, preschool and child care settings. It is written with the explicit aim of uplifting, enlightening, bringing back to basics, and reminding and reassuring early childhood educators of the main reasons they are in the profession, these being:

- for young babies and children to learn and to develop
- to ensure that our expertise in child development tracks the development, skill and learning of children in years where early intervention can make all the difference for a child's future learning
- to ensure that as educators we are teaching and children are learning.

The book is designed to give practical assistance to planning and key practices in play-based curriculum, to ensure we are being intentional in our work and to affirm the importance of early education. It will remind the community that early childhood is the most significant period of a child's life and is the foundation from which all else occurs.

In addition, this book actively acknowledges and affirms the importance of early childhood educators and their work. It provides a timely message about how the profession needs to return to the rigour of its earlier days when: clinical notes and accurate records of children's actual development and learning were kept; educators ensured that early intervention was accessed if required; that extension of skills was provided and that learning, not simply the interests of children, was planned for; and that as a profession we were respected by many other professionals.

There are many powerful studies and much research from around the world from a wide range of disciplines including psychology, neuroscience, medicine, human development and more, which highlight that the first eight years of life are indeed the most significant. Despite this, the early childhood education field continues to struggle for recognition, to articulate its high levels of expertise in the field and to reflect fully a consistent solid body of knowledge and practice across the sector. Early childhood educators have long bemoaned the fact that other educational sectors, parents and the general community have never taken seriously enough the importance of their work in early childhood. Many early childhood educators still endure the put-downs at dinner parties or other social settings of, 'So you get paid to play all day', or 'Why do you need a degree to play with kids?' There is still an overwhelming devaluing and misunderstanding of the importance of early childhood education in Australia.

The irony is that despite Federal, state and territory funding (which comes and goes), despite all the rhetoric about its importance, even from within the sector itself, the fact remains that many early childhood educators are under-qualified, underpaid and overworked. Despite the introduction and implementation of the National Early Years Framework (the Framework) (Department of Education, Employment and Workplace Relations 2009) across Australia and National Quality Standards, we are still witnessing a disturbing inconsistency of practice and confusion of expectations by educators and parents. In addition there is a lessening of actual knowledge in early childhood through the range of questionable qualifications that can be acquired through a wide range of registered training authorities (RTAs). This continues to undermine the practices in early childhood centres and to cause exhaustion, confusion and disenchantment within the profession.

Developing an educational philosophy

It is important that early childhood educators return to ensuring that evidence about children's development, learning and understandings is documented and guides practice; this being achieved by providing clinical but not cold, expert but not arrogant, and factual evidence. This is the polar opposite to the current trend of preparing hundreds of pages of artistic designed portfolios, multiple page stories about the sun shining and the sky being blue or an art gallery installation of paintings and drawings. These current trends depict little about the developing child or the skills acquired, and perhaps say more about the aspirations of the adults or current trends that miss the major point of documentation and purpose of education. Although it is important to provide accessible information to parents, the use of portfolios for documentation where every single minute of a child's experiences is written about and photographed and then displayed has increased workloads for educators to mammoth proportions. This approach to early childhood education can be seen to parallel the culture of Facebook, where the child's every moment has to be displayed and shared.

This text aims to liberate early childhood educators from feeling 'locked into' the belief that strength-based practice is all about always saying positive, lovely things about children rather than identifying as a professional practitioner when aspects of a child may require intervention, further consideration or extension.

Evidence strongly suggests that early childhood educators are often the first professionals to observe and assess or identify a child who has a potential additional need for some type of support. Early childhood educators know that teaching young children is a serious and important business. It is about identifying the needs and strengths of the developing child in what is universally acknowledged as the most important years of the lifespan.

These years are where children's self-concept, attitudes and patterns of learning, relationships and resilience, early literacy and numeracy, early development, thinking and language skills are all at critical stages. The developing brain is also at its most critical stage with neural pathways being developed, patterned and pruned depending upon the opportunities and learning that the child experiences.

Yet across the country in all areas – remote, rural, regional and inner urban – we hear example after example of early childhood educators making comments such as, 'We can't write anything about the needs of the child anymore since strength based approaches came in'; or 'We are too frightened to write anything that may be taken as a negative, even though the child really does need additional support'. Strength-based practice has become the catchphrase in early childhood education and misinterpretation of this has led to colleagues in the field, such as speech therapists and occupational therapists, commenting that, 'We used to rely on kindergarten teachers' records to help us with assessments of children. Now we seem to read the same thing about all of the children. They all have a sense of identity and community or well being!' In other words, records of children all seem to be the same, and in the vast majority of cases there is no mention of any clinical or analytical information about development, learning, literacy or numeracy. Many educators blame the Framework; others are simply confused and have lost confidence in their own initial training where development and learning, and recording astute and accurate information about children was taught (though this has now also largely gone missing in educators' training).

Many educators have reported to us that they feel guilty, and often we hear comments such as, 'We have been told development is out, that we can't refer to it anymore'. We consistently hear around Australia that early childhood educators are exhausted from the huge amounts of documentation they are keeping. In response to this we have set aside a whole chapter on planning and documentation (see Chapter 7). The message we provide in this chapter is that you do not need to document your life away – what you need to do is to get back to the rigour and basics and, as we say, 'Get you your life back!'. In Chapter 7 we provide useful strategies for how to do this. It is no coincidence that this is one of the most popular professional learning sessions we conduct across Australia. It is all about saving time, and making documentation clinical and user-friendly for educators and for families.

We must as a matter of urgency put down the camera, put down the clipboard, stop documenting moments and start living the moments. It's all about relationships: to scaffold a child to the next level of learning, to build trust, to model a skill, to facilitate future relationships, to help model empathy and to engage through play – everything is all about relationships. You cannot build relationships, be aware of moments, intuitive, wise and in tune with children's emotional needs if you are thinking about how many photos or narratives you need to write before the end of a session.

If you read nothing else in this book, please read the chapter on documentation (see Chapter 7). It aims to bring back common sense, professionalism, clinical notes and enlightenment to parents, practitioners and other colleagues.

If our main aim in transition reports is to help the child make a smooth transition into school then the Foundation teacher needs to be able to understand the report, which should be written in practical terms about the individual child, and not sound like a cloned description of every other child who has 'developed a sense of well-being, identity and communication'. Sometimes we have to take a long deep breath and remind ourselves that, with our medical, development and neuroscience backgrounds, for anyone to claim child development is 'out of favour' or 'wrong' or 'not important anymore' is nonsensical, and to believe so risks failing our duty of care in educating children.

During the 1990s a number of academics and university courses decided, in what we regard as a serious retrograde step, that culture and social influences needed to be taught above and beyond development. Of course culture, community and family have a significant impact on a child's life and learning – we are continuously reminded and respectful of this in our extensive work with Indigenous communities in the Northern Territory and Western Australia. However, it would be naïve to ignore the importance of the biology of the developing child, just as it would be naïve to ignore the importance of culture on the developing child.

This text works to bring back to life the aspects and elements of development not as a fad or an old-fashioned way of thinking about early childhood, but as a vibrant, necessary piece of evidence based on neuroscience and development. It restores rigour and analytical thinking as a major focus in the tracking and observation of children's development, learning and skill acquisition in early childhood education. Later in this chapter we present a brief account of developmentally appropriate practice and provide a synopsis of the key characteristics of development in each domain. While it is not within the scope of this book to provide detailed information about child development we have included this section as a reminder for all educators that understanding development is a critical component of personalising learning and underpins a large component of intentional teaching. Valuable resources related to child development are listed at the end of the chapter.

We are not early childhood babysitters, merely planning around children's interests to extend their interests. We are not babysitters who say to children upon arrival, 'What would you like to play with today?' We need to be intentional and well planned to ensure that learning and development is progressing. That is what education is about. That is why we are called early childhood educators!

When we understand that the brain of a young child under eight years of age is not thinking, processing or understanding in the same way as an adult, it changes everything about how we work, what we expect of children, how we set up learning play areas, how we talk with children, how we deepen relationships, how we guide their behaviours, and how we practise our profession. Using facts about the brain, and understanding the endless possibilities of the young brain while also factoring in some of the limitations, provides what is called 'evidence-based practice' rather than 'personal inclination'.

Personal inclination has long been one of the most problematic aspects in education both in primary and early childhood education. It works and sounds like this:

- 'I've always done it this way.'
- 'The parents love it and expect it this way.'
- 'I want to do it this way.'
- 'I don't agree with you.'
- 'I don't care what they said at university or at that professional development course, I'm going to do it my way.'

Personal inclination can lead to a range of dangerous practices and lowers professionalism. Here are some examples of what can happen:

- Each practitioner practices in their own way, thus there is no consistency for the young developing child as they move rooms or change educators. This leads to insecurity for the child as well as confusing messages and expectations for children and families.

- There is no culture of shared understandings, educational philosophy and subsequent practice across the centre or school, thus the practices lower the overall standard of education.
- New staff appointed are not provided with a consistent model or expectation and, therefore, new personal inclinations are commenced and the cycle of each person basically doing their own thing continues.
- Conflict frequently arises when personal inclination rather than evidence-based practices are used.
- Staff change frequently due to disharmony and inconsistency.

Ensuring consistent practice also requires strong leadership. Leaders need to understand the curriculum, and they need to be able to answer, address, model and lead the following types of key issues for staff:

- How does teaching and learning look in play-based curriculum?
- How do children learn and develop when young?
- What is play-based curriculum?
- What is the educational philosophy of the centre that drives our practice as opposed to the key values of the centre?
- Does the centre have consistent evidence-based practice?
- What place does documentation have in this centre?
- What and how do relationships and communication work with families?

Often leaders are not leading – they are simply managing situations. The leader must be clear on how the teaching and learning of young children in early childhood looks. This is one of the most defining aspects of leadership in early childhood education. The leader must seek information and grow their body of knowledge. We must remember that the National Early Years Framework is not a philosophy of education or a body of knowledge. We don't teach to the Framework and we don't teach outcomes. We teach children!

Figure 1.1 demonstrates the process for the development of an educational philosophy within an educational setting. You will notice that values are at the top; a common error in early childhood programs is that these values are mistaken for a philosophy and no further work is done on them. Values are values, and an educational philosophy is developed from the theoretical constructs and research supporting how the values are incorporated into practice. The challenge with just having statements of beliefs or values is that everyone can share the same values but interpret them into very different and varying degrees of practice in their own rooms. Therefore, working from an educational philosophy that is evidence based (not based on personal inclination) ensures that everyone in the centre works to the same philosophy and uses the same key practices.

This book is based upon theories of play and child development that over the years we have developed into what is known as Walker Learning. It is a play-based approach that has been embraced and implemented across Australia and internationally for over 20 years. It uses elements of the great traditions and theorists of child development and play, and is the very first Australian play-based curriculum to have been developed and implemented in Australia and exported onto the world stage.

Walker Learning has been developed to embrace play pedagogy not only in early childhood but into the first three years of school and beyond so that all children, regardless of where they live and what age they are, may access their universal right to play and learn and be educated. With other great educational philosophies, such as Montessori, Reggio Emilia Approach and Steiner, Walker Learning is defined by a clear educational philosophy and theory.

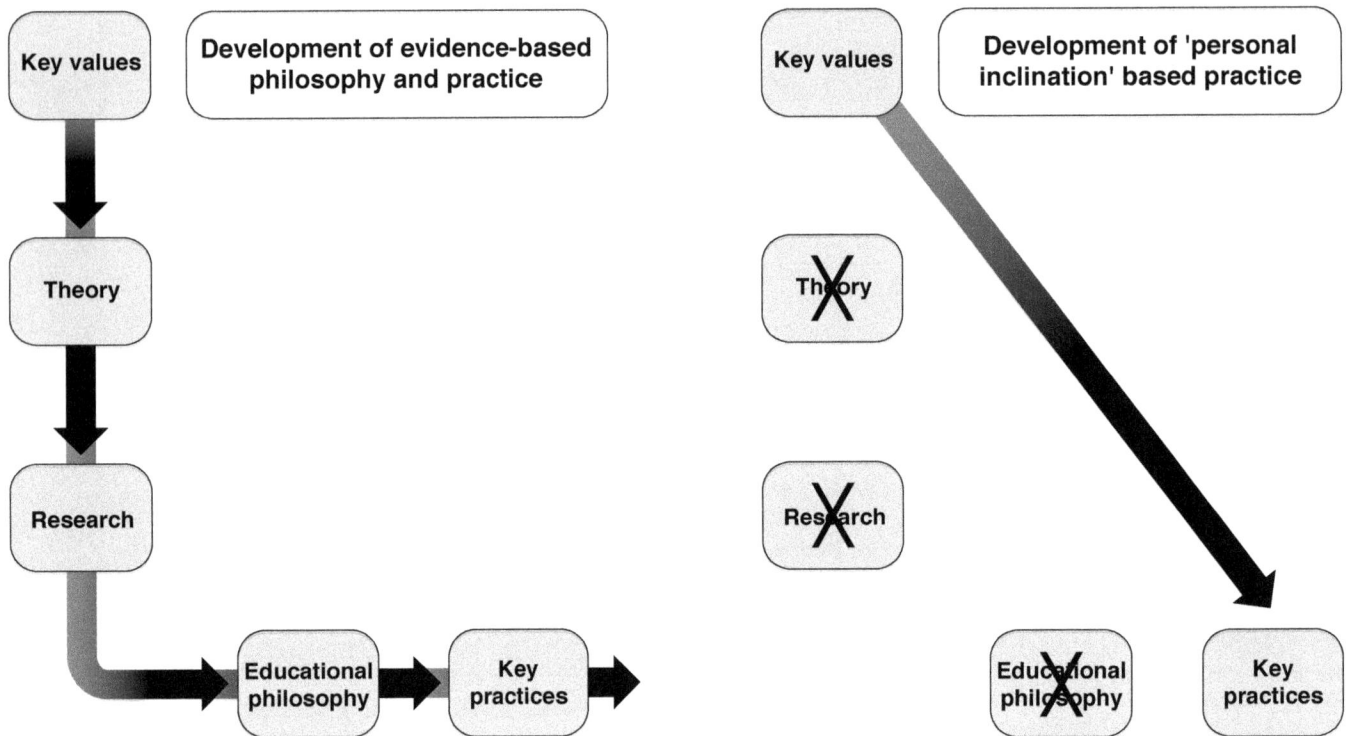

Figure 1.1 Evidence-based practice is when educators start from their key values and use theory and research to develop and validate the education philosophy that informs and guides the key practices that are consistent across the whole centre (left-hand panel).

Unfortunately, a common pathway is for educators to develop what is often called a 'philosophy' statement. This is a values statement that is then used to guide practice through personal inclination (where individual educators make their own interpretation of values and practice), with no validation from an evidence base (right-hand panel).

The uniqueness of Walker Learning is that it brings to early childhood the first Australian-based and designed, culturally appropriate play-based pedagogy that has been developed for the diverse range of Australian communities. Walker Learning embraces the concept of the 'whole child'. This concept has been around in education for many decades and has changed over time. In Walker Learning, we embrace the child holistically in terms of their overall development, using neuroscience and developmental theory as a foundation. We embrace culture, family and relationships within and beyond community as major influences in a child's life and learning.

Walker Learning accepts the diversity of children, families and cultures, and understands that all children are born with the natural ability to learn and develop by exploration, investigation and the need for explicit direction and instruction. The whole child concept includes the child as capable and an active participant in their learning alongside the adult and extended community. We view the education of a child as a systems model whereby the community, relationships and culture are all interconnected (Figure 1.2).

Chapter 8 on Walker Learning in practice describes some of the key practices that educators can use and implement in their daily practice. However, educators are free to use the planning and documentation, the intentional teaching and all other key messages within this text as part of their own existing practices.

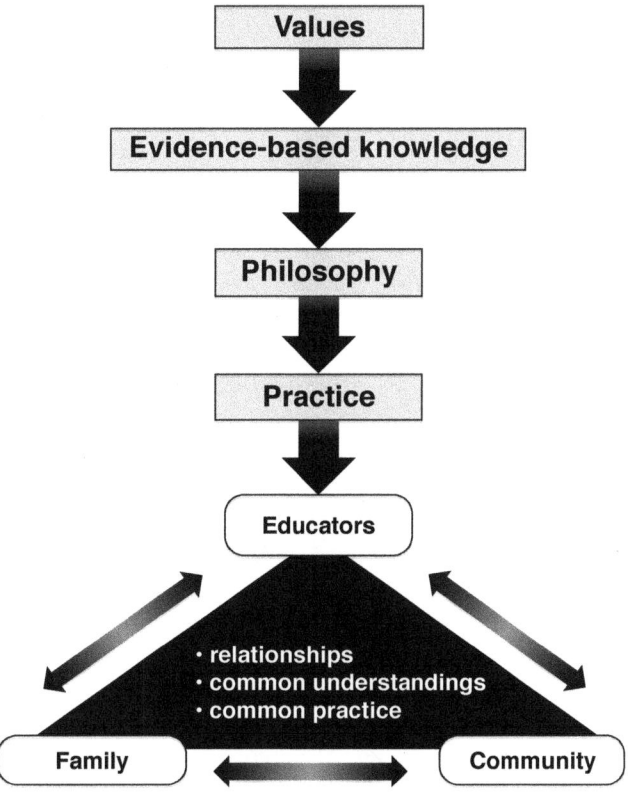

Figure 1.2 The Bass-Walker Systems Model presents a whole child and family approach to education whereby the community, relationships and culture are all interconnected. This model uses an evidence-based approach to practice.

Developmentally appropriate practice (DAP)

Developmentally appropriate practice (DAP) has been associated with early childhood and early years' education across the Western world since the 1950s (Copple & Bradekamp 2009). In recent years, alongside a range of additional perspectives of early childhood, DAP has grown and reshaped to inform practice not only within the early childhood years but right throughout the primary years. Many aspects of DAP are used as the platform for Walker Learning.

Developmentally appropriate practice is a perspective within early childhood education whereby an educator nurtures a child's social, emotional, physical and cognitive development through all practices and decisions based upon:

- theories of child development
- individually identified strengths and needs of each child uncovered through authentic assessment
- the child's cultural background as defined by community, family history and family structure (Copple & Bredekamp 2009).

In the DAP environment, children are engaged in authentic, meaningful learning experiences through intentional teaching techniques, as well as by capitalising on teachable moments. Educators do not just teach to the whole group, but use a variety of grouping strategies, including small groups, pairs and one-one-one teaching. Personalisation becomes a key component in making sure the needs and interests of each child are focused on.

Developmentally appropriate practice is based on the idea that children learn best from doing: when they are actively involved in their environment and build knowledge based on their experiences rather than through passively receiving information. Active learning environments promote hands-on learning experiences and allow children to interact with objects in their environment, as well as with their peers and educators.

The concept of DAP requires an environment offering content, materials, experiences and methodologies that are coordinated with a child's level of development and for which the individual child is ready. Children's development follows individual patterns and timing; children also vary in temperament, personality and aptitude, as well as in what they learn in their family environment and within the social and cultural contexts that shape their experiences (Marotz & Allen 2013). Three dimensions of appropriateness must be considered:

1. age appropriateness
2. individual appropriateness
3. appropriateness for the cultural and social context of the child.

The temporal pattern of children's development and learning is characterised by varying rates from child to child, as well as uneven rates across different areas of a child's individual functioning. This is discussed in detail in Chapter 3. Individual variation is subject to the:

- inevitable variability around the typical or normative course of development
- uniqueness of each child as an individual.

All children have their own strengths, needs and interests. The enormous variation in development among children of the same chronological age highlights that a child's age is only a crude index of developmental abilities and interests. For children who have special learning needs or abilities, additional efforts and resources may be necessary to optimise their development and learning. The same is true when children's prior experiences do not give them the knowledge and skills they need to thrive in a specific learning environment.

Given this normal range of variation, decisions about curriculum, teaching and interactions with children should be as individualised as possible. Rigid expectations of group norms do not reflect what is known about real differences in development and learning. At the same time, having high (but realistic) expectations for all children is essential, as is using the strategies and providing the resources necessary to help them meet these expectations.

Pedagogical best practice aligned with developmentally appropriate practice

The Walker Learning philosophy recognises that children's learning environment and development are not only influenced by biological factors, but also experiences they are exposed to in their home, cultural and community environments. This book highlights the reality that the way young children learn, and the teaching and learning strategies that are required for this learning, are unique to the early years and distinct from those of older children and adults.

The importance of understanding how child development informs personalised learning and intentional teaching

Walker Learning places a major emphasis on the maturity and development of each child. Identifying the developmental maturity of each child, and setting objectives for individuals and groups around their development, helps to focus the educator on the realities of the children in the group, and provides a framework for expectations that relate directly to the children's maturity.

Developmental domains

The developmental domains, as described on the next page, are not the same as values. This is a particularly important point as there is often confusion between a value and an aspect of maturity. For example, we may promote the value of cooperation; however, given that children are developmentally mostly in an egocentric cognitive state in the early childhood years, they are more likely to be interacting in a parallel and associative way rather than cooperatively. The following subsections provide key elements of development in each domain along with identification of developmental elements in the early years. It is important to note that developmental domains are interrelated (that is, each domain influences and is influenced by other domains); however, for clarity and the ease of observation and assessment each domain is viewed independently.

Emotional (or affective) domain

The emotional domain is the child in relation to themselves and includes:

- self-awareness
- self-concept
- self-identity/esteem/confidence
- self-regulation
- self-initiation
- independence
- separation
- attachment.

Emotional maturity includes the development of self-regulation and self-initiation; for example, 'Will I go to the pasting table?', 'What will I use?', 'What will I paste?' The development of self-expression and hence the importance of open-ended experiences (not cloned) is discussed in Chapter 5.

We usually start by looking at emotional development because that is really about the self and develops over time as the brain matures. Self-concept is not personality. Significant people in life are the primary contributors to a person's development of self-concept. It has nothing to do with genetics. When a child is born, they have no self-awareness. The development of self (self-concept) is formed by two major sets of people in a child's life – parents and educators. Educators and parents are modelling messages, and these have a huge impact on a child's self-concept. Peers start to influence concept of self from about Year 6, but for most of the life span it is parents and educators who are the most influential. Strategies for strengthening a child's sense of self are discussed in Chapter 4 on communication, and include:

- encouragement rather than praise
- 'I' messages
- reflective listening
- separating the child from the behaviour.

Social domain

The social domain is the child (themself) in relation to the other, and includes:

- tolerating views of others
- relationships with others
- peer association and interest
- empathic socialisation (cognitive)
- friendship (reciprocal – emotional connection)
- approaching/initiating contact with others
- expression of views with others
- parallel play/associative/cooperative.

Social maturity develops over time and is much more than whether a child has a friend or is able to play with others. Stage of social development also reflects stages of cognition. The early childhood years are characterised by children being in a very egocentric world – that's why we want children to investigate their world from their perspective, develop their fine motor skills, have practice working and playing beside others in parallel and associative play, and develop oral language.

Cognitive domain

The cognitive domain is the child thinking about their thinking, and includes:

- problem solving
- lateral and divergent thinking
- creative thinking
- questioning
- exploration of understanding the properties of objects

- understandings from within and one's immediate world to the wider world (corresponding with brain development)
- creative expression
- concentration span
- taking in information
- following directions
- making sense of
- reasoning
- symbolic thinking for more mature children
- perspective taking
- moral development (rules).

Cognitive development is all about thinking, perceiving and reasoning. It is closely related to language. It includes the wide range of aspects of thinking – how the brain is developing – the development of empathy, becoming less egocentric, being able to become more symbolic in one's thinking and growing in greater awareness of the wider world. Around the age of eight years, something amazing happens in the cerebral cortex ... empathic understanding begins to develop.

Language domain

The language domain generally relates to oral language and includes:

- development of speech pronunciation
- grammar
- vocabulary
- comprehension
- speaking and listening
- self-expression
- expression of wants and needs/emotional.

Physical domain

The physical domain includes:

- gross motor skills
- fine motor sills
- bilateral coordination
- spatial awareness
- strength
- aerobic fitness
- physical health
- body proportions and body composition
- body image
- exercise
- nutrition.

Table 1.1 outlines the various development elements of children in the early childhood years.

Factors related to development

Factors related to development include:

- Development occurs generally in an orderly sequence, although some elements of individual, family and cultural experiences also impact on temporal patterns of growth and development.
- Children are active learners, drawing on direct physical and social experiences.
- Play is the most important vehicle for children's emotional, social and cognitive development.

Table 1.1 Development elements of children in the early childhood years

Social/emotional	Cognition	Language	Physical
• Self-help skills • Egocentric world • Attachment/separation issues • Self-concept • Self-regulation • Self-initiation • Independence • Self-expression • Initiating contact with others • Working and playing alongside others • Early conflict resolution	• Egocentric • Limited concentration span • Following directions two to three at a time (maximum) • Making sense of the world through concrete examples • Creative/imaginative experiences promote understanding of their experience • Limited understanding of time, space and perspective • Thinking and perceiving/reasoning (closely related to language) • Lack of empathy – cerebral cortex developing in first eight years • Difficulty in predicting ahead • Process orientation rather than future planning and end product	• Speaking and listening • Articulation and pronunciation • Growth of vocabulary • Comprehension greater than vocabulary • Difficult to express needs and wants • Self-talk promotes thinking	• Handedness being determined • Body/bilateral coordination becoming refined • Spatial awareness developing • Fine motor/eye–hand coordination • Gross motor • Vision and peripheral vision still maturing • Tiredness and need for approximately 11 hours sleep

Examples of developmental practice using Walker Learning

These are some of the ways developmental practice is evidenced in Walker Learning.

- Tables do not dominate the physical environment as the major focus of the room. Contained, defined spaces for children are established.
- The environment provides defined spaces and individual learning play areas, as well as opportunities for children to work alongside each other.
- To a considerable degree, children are able to self-regulate, self-select and act independently within the learning environment without having to have all materials, resources and equipment provided by the educator.
- Individual records and observation are taken of the children both in relation to learning objectives and their development.
- The educator provides opportunities for individual interests.
- Children's development and learning is viewed as the main starting point for planning learning intentions.
- Children's culture, family, and individual strengths and needs are built into the range of experiences provided.
- Inclusive language and diversity are promoted through the integration of books, the language used by educators and the resources provided.
- Creative and open-ended experiences are the major strategies used for engagement and teaching.

- The use of outdoor space provides connectedness and continuity with the indoor experiences, along with being an area in its own right. As with the indoor environment, the outdoor environment is developed with intention (related to development, learning and children's interests) and the use of provocations.
- Active hands-on learning through play is the major tool for teaching and learning.
- Time is provided for children to engage in their learning and gain a sense of achievement.
- A variety of learning play areas (experiences), including dramatic play, construction, collage, sensory, tinkering, carpentry, painting/drawing, science/nature, literacy resource and numeracy resource are available throughout each session.
- Time for physical and quiet experiences is embedded throughout the day.
- Reflection of children's own learning is integrated into each day.
- Intrinsic motivation is a key aspect of Walker Learning. Extrinsic rewards, stickers and stars are not used.
- Assessment is based on observation, samples of work and individual records.
- Parents are encouraged to participate in the learning with their children.
- The educator scaffolds, responds to and directs children through their learning experiences.

Summary

This chapter describes the key aims of this book, which are to:

- empower early childhood educators to renew themselves in professionalism, their body of knowledge and evidence-based practice
- provide practical support for documentation, play learning areas, relationship building and clarity around our key purposes in early childhood education
- provide opportunities for reflection on practice
- provide a model for play-based learning that is developmentally and culturally appropriate.

Suggested resources

Copple, C & Bredekamp, S (eds) 2009, *Developmentally appropriate practice in early childhood programs: serving children from birth through age 8*, National Association for the Education of Young Children, Washington, DC.

Marotz, LR & Allen, KE 2013, *Developmental profiles: pre-birth through adolescence*, 7th edn, Wadsworth, Belmont, CA.

Chapter 2

Intentional teaching: it's everything and all we do, all of the time

'It is the supreme art of the teacher to awaken joy in creative expression and knowledge.'

Albert Einstein

Introduction

Early childhood educators educate; we don't babysit, entertain, organise activities or merely set up a range of children's current interests to occupy them for a few hours each day or week. The term 'educate' is used in a holistic way to include the child's development, culture, academic, conceptual understanding and skill acquisition appropriate to their age, stage of life and context.

The education of a child is highly complex and requires not only the family and community but also the role of specialised staff (early childhood educators) who have expert knowledge about the early years of life. Early childhood educators who hold this specialised knowledge understand how young children grow, develop and learn and also how to facilitate further growth, skill and learning.

Through the lens of the expert eye, educators are able to assess the child's rate of development and maturation, how young children are acquiring skills, learning and understanding concepts, developing language and comprehension, moving through different stages of early literacy and numeracy concepts, developing their own sense of self, resilience, socialisation, emotional maturity and, of course, a deep and broad range of elements of skill.

The expert early childhood educator understands the challenges of behaviours, the emotional needs and rivalries between children, the complexities of emotions and the wonderful curiosities and brilliance of children's imaginations, and the need for exploration of children's perspectives and roles beyond their own. This expertise and knowledge provides a strong platform for being intentional for children's development, skills and learning.

It is therefore imperative that early childhood educators reclaim this expertise as the absolute foundational starting point for all that occurs both proactively and in response to children's interactions, investigations and behaviours.

To reclaim, embrace and endorse this expert body of knowledge is now of great urgency – this is the very essence of the early childhood education profession. Unfortunately, too often it is absent, and has been displaced by the misguided practice of only extending children's interests or engaging children in projects such as sustainability or snails or dinosaurs. Doing projects/topics similar to what is often offered at primary school, or researching/extending a child's interest, is totally missing the major purpose and aim of early childhood education.

Educators do not start the day or their planning or their environment set-up based upon children's interests. Educators do not plan to have adult-led and designed 'projects/topics' for three and four year olds, nor should children have to endure the projects, topics and themes that will be replicated through the first five years of primary school.

> *We believe this phenomenon of projects and interest-based planning has become the greatest mistake, myth, error and grave concern to have occurred in early childhood education for many decades (other than the fixation on photos and portfolios).*

The starting point of all planning for early childhood education (and in fact for a child of any age) is: (1) where is this child at developmentally and in their learning; (2) what is next, or where to next, for this child; and (3) how do I engage this child in a learning experience that is open-ended and focused on skill acquisition and process (not outcome)? This is what intention is all about and it is discussed in the next sections. The process for planning and documenting with intention is discussed in Chapter 7.

What does intention mean in relation to education in early childhood?

Intentional teaching is when the educator has purpose, with specific goals, knowledge and aims in mind in order to facilitate and scaffold the development, learning, skills and concepts of children in their early childhood years of education. Intentional teaching and learning in early childhood education is about skills and much less about content. This does not mean we do not provide children with lots of new opportunities and exposures to learn about their community and world, but we concentrate on the neurological facts regarding what children need to be acquiring in their early years (this is discussed in Chapter 3).

Enormous confusion reigns about what intentional teaching and learning actually means. Some of the comments we have heard across the profession include:

- 'This is the intentional teaching side of the room and the other is our free play side.'
- 'We have intentional teaching and play in the inside and free play outside.'
- 'We have intentional teaching in the morning and then free play after lunch and rest.'
- 'We don't plan anything intentional at the start. We wait to see what children are interested in or what they choose from the cupboard or shed.'
- 'We let the children choose, we don't plan ahead.'

These comments and messages should sound the alarm bells across the profession. None of these would be acceptable in any other sector or stage of education and they are certainly not appropriate in early childhood education. The confusion has come about due to the less than satisfactory wording that surrounds some of the National Early Years Framework terminology and the mixed messages coming out of some early childhood training institutions.

Developing intentional teaching in early childhood

Intention in education just doesn't happen – educators need to 'intentionally' develop intention in everything they do; in their relationships with children, in their planning, in the learning environment set-up, in their interactions and scaffolding, and in their responsiveness to children and the experiences. Intentional is both proactive and responsive.

This section examines how intention is developed in a number of key areas.

Intentional relationships between educators and children

Relationships are one of our major intentions. We know that for young children particularly, relationships are the most critical element of survival, trust, motivation, emotional security, growth, physical thriving, development of pro-social behaviours, and the list goes on. For young children under two years, attachment and primary carers are imperative.

So, using intention the key considerations include:

- Do the babies and toddlers have a primary caregiver who is assigned intentionally and who proactively undertakes this role?
- Does the primary caregiver ensure they are the main contact and relationship with the family and child?
- Does the centre intentionally consider consistent staffing for babies and toddlers in at least a two-year cycle for trust and consistent relationships between children and educators?

Additional relationship intentions are:

- Do educators have additional professional development in working and understanding specific age groups so they build expertise and a body of knowledge?
- Are educators provided with professional development on how to effectively communicate with each other and to enhance communication with children and families?
- Does the centre intentionally work on building the same staff relationships together so they work harmoniously and professionally together?
- Does the centre proactively and intentionally provide for siblings to be together for large chunks of each day to continue to foster sibling and family relationships?
- Does the centre refrain from moving babies and toddlers into another room just because they have had a birthday and therefore lose their primary attachment with staff and children?

Intentional planning

Planning is one of the most important elements where intention is imperative. Planning does not start with the child's interests; it starts with our expert body of knowledge. Chapter 7 on planning and documentation works through this process in detail, but it is important to mention it briefly here in relation to intention.

When we first start a year with children, wherever we may be in the country, or if we are in a region for the first time, we may not know the local cultures, community or interests of children. What we can rely on, however, is the body of expert knowledge on play theory, child development theory and the open-ended nature of the play-based curriculum. It is this area of expertise that helps immeasurably with intentional teaching and learning in early childhood.

We don't need to know the children to start planning with intention. We know in general terms the types of play, experiences, resources, materials and how to set them up that provoke interests, exploration, practice, investigation and manipulation of these objects dependent upon the age of the children. Through our expert body of knowledge we can plan to set up a broad range of experiences that will engage, enhance and expose children intentionally to further exploration and learning.

This is one of our most basic, but most important, insurance policies as early childhood educators. We are ensuring that our learning environments and planning are intentional for the education and learning of the child, not for extending the interests of the child.

An intentional learning environment

Our body of knowledge about children and their development and our expertise in play-based curriculum theory enables us to set up learning play areas that reflect, enhance and extend children in a range of areas for learning and skill in creative and engaging open-ended experiences. All of these experiences are intentionally developed in regard to the materials, resources, how we place them, why we put them there and what we call the provocations (ideas, prompts, tools, fuel for further thinking, talking, manipulation, exploration, investigation).

These are all open for the children to take wherever they want, thus providing for the interests and ideas of each child. It is also intentional in that we, as the experts, know that at the same time, skill, concepts, learning and development will be occurring.

Sometimes this learning will be occurring simply by the type of provocations we have intentionally placed in each area, and sometimes by the scaffolding of the educator's language and modelling. These provocations, materials and resources should be appropriate to the child's stage of maturity, empower children to extend and explore further, be suitable for mixed age groupings if required, always honour what and how the child wishes to explore and interact, and have no hidden adult agenda in terms of what should be made or how it should look. The only adult agenda is that the intention is for learning and education – there is no hidden agenda!

These provocations do not require children to make the same thing, copy an adult-made artefact or adult-designed model. The learning play areas use only open-ended materials where children can use their own imaginations to create and explore and master in any way they wish.

Likewise, the learning play areas should not include stencilled cut-outs, shape cutters in play-dough areas or colouring-in sheets or formal alphabet tracing sheets. In Chapter 6, on setting up the learning play areas and environment, we work our way through this in more detail.

The important point here is that in intentional teaching in play-based curriculum the materials, resources and provocations are intentionally set up with skills, development and learning in the mind of the educators. It is completely up to the children how they then engage and utilise these resources in open-ended ways. It is the nature, depth, range and attention to detail of these provocations that need greater attention in early childhood education. This is discussed in Chapter 6.

Interactions and scaffolding is intentional

As educators we always have a choice. We can sit in the dramatic play area and ask for another piece of chocolate cake or we can ask the four year old the following:

- 'How many pieces have I already eaten and how many more do you think you might make today?'
- 'Will you be selling any and how much might they cost?'
- 'Do we need to make some money?'
- 'What type of shop might sell cupcakes?'

Our language modelling of new words, our extension of concepts such as 'more', 'shopping', 'money', 'costs', is one of the imperatives in intentional teaching. This is how in dramatic play, for example, so much rich and rigorous learning takes place.

> *Perspective, language, thinking and concepts of just about anything in the world can be modelled in the educator's language – mathematical, literacy, science, social skills, the list is endless. The interactions and scaffolding of the educator through language and provocations is extremely rich and important.*

The key is that the educator cannot use intentional interactions and language if they are unclear as to what their intentions actually are for each child. Of course the educator can scaffold in response to children's spontaneous actions and behaviours, but the key to working and responding so as to personalise learning for each child is to be very clear about each individual child's stage of development, and to be intentional and clear about what each child needs in the way of extension, intervention and modelling.

This is where starting from the simplistic notion of a child's interest misses the vital elements of the educator's key purpose.

> *We are not there to extend an interest. We are there to move a child's learning forward: to grow in our own awareness of their skills, needs and strengths and to scaffold and extend these – not their interests.*

During transition times, at snack times, in our spontaneous chats with children, indeed at all times, we need to be thinking hard about what and who we are as a model for grammar, for conversation, for pronunciation, for speaking and listening, for eye contact, for smiling, for engagement and for appropriate general communication skills. We are intentionally modelling effective communication skills between ourselves and other educators. We are intentionally self-aware and self-managing. This is discussed in more detail in Chapter 4 on communication.

Proactive and responsive intention

At this stage, we have planned, we have set up the learning environments, we have discussed with our colleagues and we have intentions in mind. We know where the children are in their skills and aspects of development. We are prepared with the sorts of scaffolding we think we might provide for each child on a particular day. We have incorporated their unique interests or life into our conversations and sometimes added these into our learning play areas.

We have organised the day or session, perhaps prioritised particular focus children we wish to spend additional time with, or have perhaps read up on our clinical records on these children so our information about them is fresh in our minds and our intentions are very clear (see Chapter 7), proactive, organised and ready for the day.

This is what proactive intention is about. It is not about discussing with colleagues how many photos we need for each child's portfolio. It is not about who will type up a daily reflection near the end of the day and leave the room to do so. It is not about who will wash the tables down or simply who will set up outside.

Intention is about why we set up what we do set up outside and the type of language we might use outside when children are climbing over the obstacle course. We might have decided intentionally to model the language of mathematical location, such as 'over, under, through, between, on top, underneath, on the side'. Frighteningly, in our work as educators, we see very few plans that have this type of language and mathematical intention.

All of this is called *proactive prepared intention*. As an educator, you have aims, purpose and clarity. You know why, what and who you are focusing on, and you have knowledge about the children to assist you in educating, scaffolding, extending and supporting them.

Responsive intention

One of the greatest things about young children is that we never know what they will create, how they will use the materials we have placed out for them, what they will decide to do with them, the processes they will use, or where their energy, creativity and explorations will take them on any given day or moment. So, the educator must use their expertise to respond to this wonderful spontaneity, in what is called responsive intention and scaffolding.

We may have anticipated some of the children using the dramatic play area as a hospital when we set it up with white shirts, stethoscopes, etc. However, they decided to turn it into a vet clinic. The skill in intentional teaching and learning is to scaffold the skills and understandings in the vet clinic and to add provocations associated with the vet clinic that are related to skills and understandings. This does not mean that educators should fall into the trap of making all the children do a project about 'vets'.

Intention for process not project

Intentional teaching is not to make all children learn a hundred facts about vets, or mini beasts, or snails, or water sustainability, or the Antarctic. In fact, as Chapter 3 on neuroscience will show and describe, young children don't capture and retain or make sense of this type of 'content'. They can repeat it, but they don't really make sense of it. This is often called an adult pleaser type of project as it often looks substantial and more sophisticated than a few boxes stuck together. However, as we will discuss, early childhood intentional teaching and learning is about skills, and not so much about content. This is extremely important to note.

So, if the hospital becomes a vet, it is the roles, the interactions, the taking of appointments, the writing of illness and injuries, the oral language, the taking turns, the perspectives and roles taken, the negotiations, the posters and texts, the labels and writing, the taking the temperature of the animals, the fine motor skills of the bandaging that becomes the major scaffold and focus, not making all the children find out every single thing they can about a vet.

Remember once they get to school, children will be doing projects about vets and myriad other topics for many years!

Intentional teaching in early childhood must pitch itself to the neurological stage of the child. It must scaffold the developmental skills, the processes, a little of the roles and perspectives; but it must not miss the skills and launch into a full-scale project about content and a topic. That is a traditional primary school theme, and even schools are doing this less and less.

Fact check: busting the myths

Fact check 1

In early childhood education throughout history, we have always incorporated the culture, family life, context and interests of children as a form of respect and as a leaping-off point or opportunity to engage the learner to acquire a skill or further learning or exposure.

- We don't plan for interests for the interest's sake.
- We don't extend interests for the interest's sake (that is what a good babysitter does).

Using some element of a child's life as part of planning is not new. However, thinking that our starting point in planning or as part of intentional teaching is all about children's interests is wrong and inappropriate.

Fact check 2

Our planning, our scaffolding, our work with children is all about intention! What skill, what aspect of development or learning, and what aspect of behaviours or interaction are we wanting to extend, support, promote and assess?

These are the questions that intention drives us to ask and consider every single day.

Fact check 3

The *wrong* question is, 'What is this child's interest and how can I extend it?'

The *right* question is, 'What do I know about this child in relation to skill, or development or learning and how can I move this child forward?'

The right question is intentional and is asked as an educator.

The wrong question is like a good babysitter wanting to engage and entertain the child for a while.

Fact check 4

All we do in education is intentional. Whatever situation we find ourselves in, everything is intentional. It can either be proactive or responsive; planned or spontaneous.

Intentional teaching and learning in early childhood uses open-ended play-based curriculum as its basis. It does not use projects like themes, and it uses as its major emphasis, that wonderful phrase, 'It is the process not the end product': it is the process of developing skills and learning and promoting development that is most important.

It requires the educators to know children in terms of development and skill. It requires clinical and accurate records of individual children and their development and learning including literacy and numeracy.

It does not place an emphasis upon children's interests, but simply includes the lives of children and their interests, culture, family and community as one part of their overall context for learning.

Intentional teaching and learning must include development of the child. This understanding continues to be a worldwide movement and the reality is that we are, as well as being cultural and social beings, also biological and neurological. There is little point in arguing whether we are one or the other, as we are both. Educators must intentionally plan, document, implement and teach with this in mind, proactively and responsively all the time. That is what it means to be an early childhood educator.

Summary

The key aims of this chapter are to show that:

- the education of the child should always be intentional
- intention is both proactive and responsive
- intention is at times spontaneous
- intention includes all aspects of development, learning and skill acquisition – the whole child
- the interests of children are a secondary consideration in planning, not a starting point
- we extend learning, not interests
- interests, culture, family and life are part of the child, as are their development, neurology and personality.

Suggested resource

Epstein, AS 2007, *The intentional teacher: choosing the best strategies for young children's learning*, National Association for the Education of Young Children, Washington, DC.

Chapter 3
Neuroscience informing evidence-based practice

'The beginning of something is always important, especially when it is young and needs time.'

Plato

Introduction

Early childhood educators have one of the most important jobs in the world – a fact that is rarely acknowledged or celebrated in the profession, let alone by media or outside the profession. What is the evidence to make such a claim? The evidence is that a child's early childhood experience has a significant influence on success in their future life – this is not only educational success, but also the increased opportunity to be successful in more aspects of life ranging from financial security, family stability and reduction of crime. This claim has been documented and confirmed by numerous high-powered, long-term studies, including the Canadian Early Years Study (Akbari & McCuaig 2014), High Scope (Schweinhart & Weikart 1997) and more recently the Effective Provision of Pre-School Education Project (EPPE) (Sylva et al. 2004). These data show that next to the influence of parents (in most cases the mother), a child's early childhood education experience is the next strongest predictor for success in education and life opportunity. Given the importance of early childhood education it is imperative that early childhood education pedagogy is underpinned by evidence-based practice.

Developmental neuroscience and psychology are the key fields that provide the evidence base for early childhood practice. To provide a child-centred pedagogy that personalises learning for each child requires the understanding of individual children – their family, culture and religion – and, importantly, where the child is developmentally and what is appropriate practice for that child relative to their development and stage of learning.

Understanding some critical elements of developmental neuroscience and psychology is critical to inform pedagogical practice which helps to provide developmentally appropriate practice and sets each child up for success. The educator needs to provide a pedagogy that develops all the key skills children at a particular age need for their development, and to be able to pitch the learning so that each child is truly engaged, learning is contextual and the child is challenged so that they are extended and experience some form of success. In this chapter we provide a synopsis of the developmental aspects of brain development and how these inform practice. In this way, the chapter provides the evidence base for rigorous early childhood pedagogy.

Nature and nurture: not all children are born equal

Not all children are born 'equal' – if they were, they would all be the same height, and have the same skin and eye colour and the same temperament. We all know this is not the case – and the appreciation of each individual child in their own right is the fulcrum of all child-centred practice. Providing equity to all children is to understand and respect diversity and difference. The genetic (nature) and environment (nurture) debate too often gets side-tracked by professionals' inclinations to a particular field of study – the socio-culturists not honouring the influence of biology and the biologists not honouring the impact of the environment, for example. As with all living things on earth, development is the result of interaction between biology and environment. The interactionist model dismisses personal inclination and acknowledges that genetic, biological and environmental influences all have significant influences on the way a child develops as their own unique person.

When a child is conceived they have their own unique genetic transcript (or blueprint) – this is known as their 'genotype'. The environment influences how genes will operate and function (or be expressed) and the outcome is known as an individual's 'phenotype'. The environment influences how an individual's genes respond and has a significant impact on an individual's ability to reach their full genetic potential. The study of epigenetics reveals that even the environment of grandparents and parents may influence a child's genetic template, even before they are conceived. The environment in the womb also influences genetic expression. However, the most important environmental influence on a child's genetic expression is during the early childhood years.

The common analogy used to explain the interactionist model is that of two seeds of exactly the same genetic transcript – the growth of each seed into a seedling and then an adult plant is influenced by the nutrients in the soil, the amount of water and sun it receives, and varying weather events. So even though both seeds have the same starting point, the environment plays a significant role in determining whether each seed can reach its full genetic potential.

Building on this analogy one would expect that the mission of all early childhood educators would be to provide each child with a rich and personalised environment that enables opportunities for each child to optimise their individual potential.

Each child has their own unique starting point, their own unique potential and their own unique sequence and pattern of growth and development. In addition, the way each child perceives and processes information is unique. The interactionist model honours and values each child's uniqueness and understands the importance of the environment to give every child the greatest opportunity to optimise their unique potential. It is the challenge of the educator to be perceptive to each child's uniqueness and to pitch opportunities that are just right for that child, depending on where they are developmentally and how they process information and learn from experiences.

Ignoring genetic predisposition, therefore, or assuming that only environment impacts upon the developing child or influences learning, or that cultural experiences alone promote learning, are incorrect assumptions. For instance, an individual's genetic predisposition to temperament is present at birth, before parenting or influence of environment has any impact. Influences and messages from key environments and people impact upon behaviours and potential. But temperament remains reasonably constant throughout life.

Brain development: 100 billion neurons and building

The human brain is a remarkable organ – nothing on earth is comparable to it in relation to capacity, complexity, function and sophistication. When a child is born the brain contains on average 100 billion neurons, which is a similar number of neurons and connections to the adult brain. Despite this starting point, a baby's brain is only partly constructed, as 83 per cent of the brain's networks are yet to be constructed. This process of growing the brain's network involves single neurons making connections and wiring together with neighbouring neurons. Ten thousand connections per neuron is typical but this figure can go as high as 15 000 connections and even 100 000 connections before the wiring of the network is complete. The time of greatest activity for this building of connectivity is in the early childhood years and puberty; however, the major construction of the brain continues into the early twenties with further fine-tuning occurring for approximately another 30 years.

The development of neural connections in the brain is not all about making more and more connections, but rather is a process of continual landscaping, with rapid outgrowth and connections occurring alongside furious pruning back of other connections. The growth and pruning are the result of experiences, learning and constant rewiring (neural plasticity). For instance, when babies are born their brains have about the same number of connections as adults have, but by the time they are three years old, the connections in specific regions have doubled or even tripled. Pruning takes place and by the time they are eight years old, they are back to adult numbers. This happens again in puberty, but in quite different regions (Medina 2012).

Neural plasticity is how the brain responds to stimulus or lack of stimulus – that is, how the brain grows or is 'pruned back' as a result of everyday experiences. This extensive malleability and plasticity of the brain in the early years has often led to the misunderstanding that this should be the time to introduce formal education – to start formally structured learning – even to the point of teaching children to read at three months of age! Understanding this phase of brain development and the implications for pedagogy is a critical part of evidence-based practice in the early childhood years.

Executive function skills: skills for success in life

Evidence clearly shows that this time of extensive neural growth and plasticity is directly related to the development of many other skills, but not the formal learning of numeracy and literacy. Recent research has documented that during this phase of life the greatest development is related to executive function skills. Executive functioning controls planning, foresight, problem solving and goal setting.

A child's executive function is a critical component of intellectual prowess. Executive function skills are built over time and are highly interrelated (each type of skill utilises elements of the others). Executive function skills support the process of learning (the *how* to learn).

There are three major categories of executive function skills (Center on the Developing Child 2011).

1. Inhibitory control – this is our ability to control impulses, and to master and filter our thoughts so we can resist temptations, distractions and habits, and pause and think before we act.

2. Working memory – this is the capacity to hold and manipulate information in our heads over short periods of time, to make plans, remember, and work with rules and functions.

3. Cognitive flexibility – this is the capacity to adjust to changing demands, priorities or perspectives, and to maintain focus despite distractions.

The sequence of development of the executive functioning skills shows that from birth to six to eight years of age is the most critical time for the development of working memory, inhibitory control and cognitive/mental flexibility (see Figure 3.1).

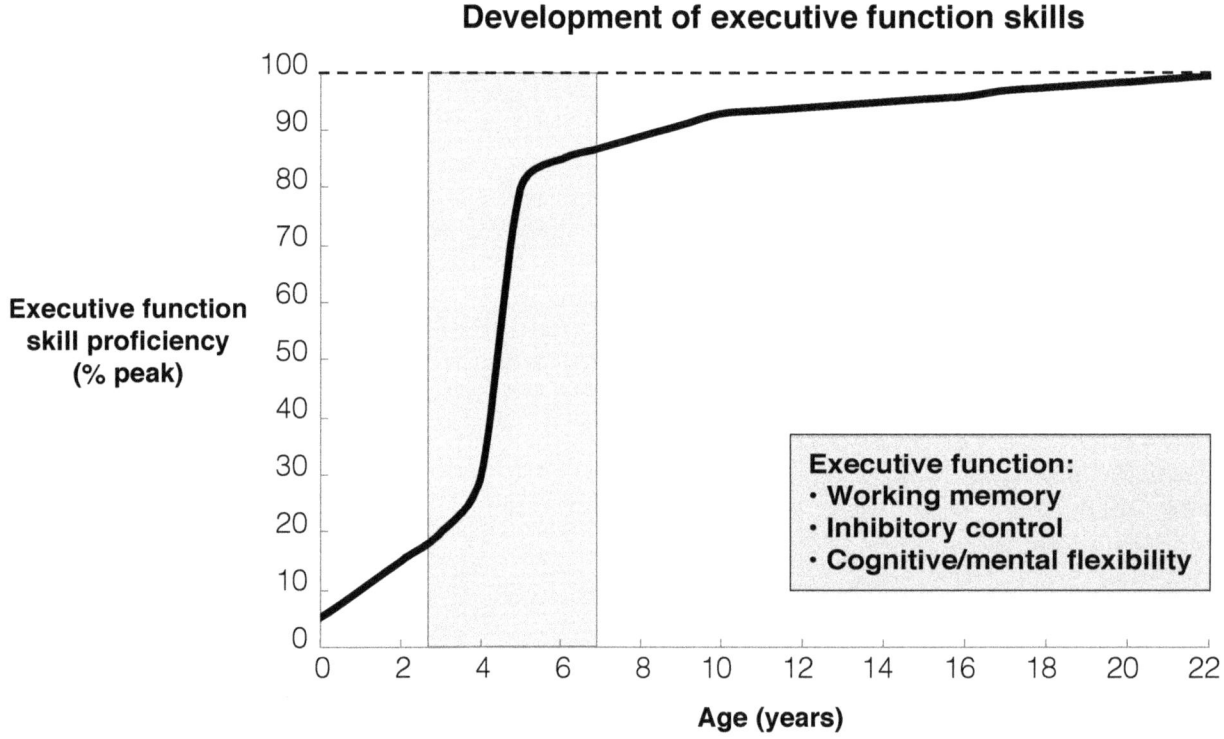

Figure 3.1 The sequence of development of the executive functioning skills by age. This shows that from birth to six to eight years of age is the most critical time for the development of working memory, inhibitory control and cognitive/mental flexibility. (Adapted from Center on the Developing Child 2011, p. 5.)

Executive function skills are crucial building blocks for the early development of both cognitive and social capabilities. Like all skills, the development of executive function has a genetic component – each individual has an innate transcript that regulates how and when these skills develop. However, the optimal development of these skills requires a supportive environment that provides children with the opportunity to explore, self-regulate and practise those emerging skills while being supported and scaffolded by an adult. As the child masters aspects of the skills, the adult allows more independence and then provides a more sophisticated scaffold to extend the skills.

Acquiring the foundations of these skills during early childhood is one of the most important components of child development. As seen in Figure 3.2, the formative development of brain regions associated with executive function occurs in early childhood. The platform of these skills allows the child to build on these fundamental capabilities through middle childhood and adolescence.

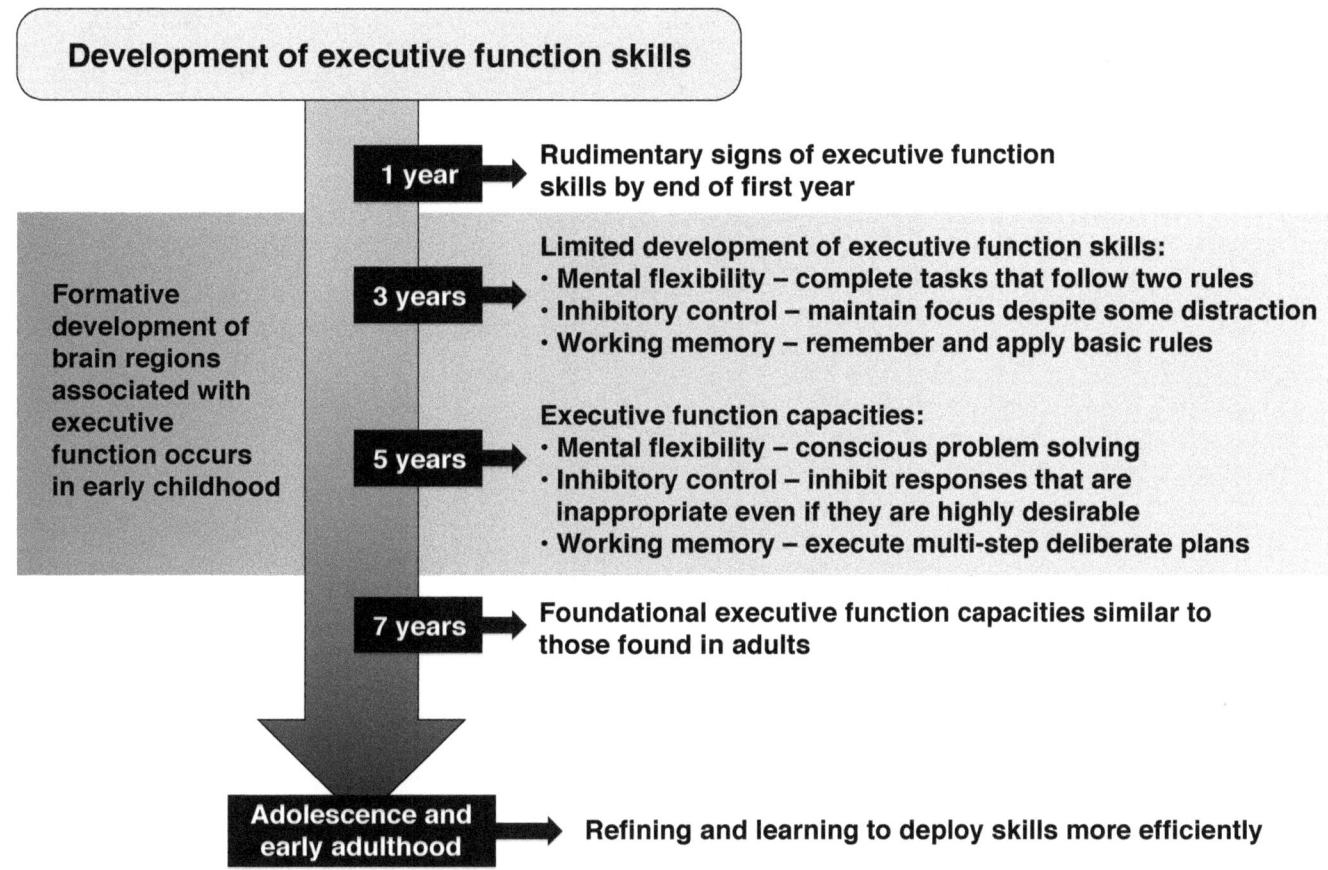

Figure 3.2 Acquiring the foundations of executive function skills during early childhood is one of the most important components of child development. (Adapted from Center on the Developing Child 2011, p. 4.)

Executive functions underpin the development of a broad range of skills, competencies and behaviours, including learning academically and social interaction. High executive function is one of the two greatest predictors of academic success that exist in the research literature (Medina 2014, p. 135). Moreover emotional regulation – controlling impulses – provides a very powerful predictor of cognitive performance. The inextricable link between intellectual capacities and emotional processing, and subsequent implications for learning and development are only now being appreciated and have significant implications in early childhood education. These data underpin the importance of providing an environment that fosters the healthy development of these skills. Correspondingly, environments that do not facilitate this skill development can contribute to long-term difficulties for children.

Extended exposure to threatening and stressful situations can compromise the development and deployment of executive functioning skills.

Exposure to highly stressful early environments has been reported to be associated with deficits in the development of children's working memory, attention and inhibitory control skills (Lengua, Honorado & Bush 2007; Maughan & Cicchetti 2002; O'Connor et al. 2000). Chronic stressful and chaotic environments make it difficult for children to engage their executive functioning skills – even in situations such as the preschool where they may be safe (Liston et al. 2006; Liston, McEwen & Casey 2009).

Young children who have problems staying focused and resisting urges to respond impulsively not only have trouble in school but have trouble following directions generally and are at elevated risk of displaying aggressive and confrontational behaviour with adults and other children (Center on the Developing Child 2011). Children who exhibit difficulties with self-regulation often have very challenging behaviour and require particularly sensitive and intuitive adult support. Children who have not developed foundations in executive functioning skills often find it difficult to engage in play with other children; they are often told what to do, are isolated or behave in a way that causes the play to break down.

As discussed in the previous section, maturation of neural pathways has a large individual variability – this is also the case for the development of executive functioning skills. A typical scenario may be one where a child has good skills in focusing attention and managing distractions but may not be so well developed in working memory. In developmentally appropriate practice the role of the educator is to determine the stage of development of executive functioning skills of each child that will then guide the educator's support and scaffolding for the child.

Rigorous early childhood pedagogy embraces the complex integrations that are apparent among executive functioning, social competence and academic skills. The opportunity to develop these skills is presented through a social constructivism model where children learn through doing, and practising in real, relevant and meaningful ways. The learning is scaffolded by the adult and is integrated so that the learning of all three domains is embedded through a child's natural play – so that the pedagogy is not a series of silos that have no connection to each other or the child. The pedagogy is underpinned by child-directed play that is intentionally scaffolded by the adult.

Also of interest is that executive function skills compose a large component of a child's readiness for school, including being able to:

- separate from their primary caregiver
- make decisions
- avoid distractions
- self-initiate
- maintain focus and engagement
- manage emotions – self-regulate
- communicate wants and needs verbally – individually and in front of a group
- problem solve
- seek help
- have basic independence skills.

Academic prowess or ability is not an indicator for school readiness; rather, school readiness is about social and emotional maturity and the development of executive function skills. Early childhood education is a curriculum in its own right; it is not the year to 'prepare children for school'. On the contrary, the early childhood experience is to support, scaffold and extend children to develop these skills along their own innate trajectory to optimise their own potential.

The power of social and emotional skills

The most recent Organisation for Economic Co-operation and Development (OECD) project, titled 'Skills for social progress: the power of social and emotional skills', was released in March 2015 and highlights the significance of building social and emotional skills into curriculum, alongside literacy and numeracy (OECD 2015). It is pleasing to finally access empirical data showing evidence of how critical these elements are in the teaching and learning process.

The development of social and emotional skills has a significant effect on a child's future prospects.

The development of a child's cognitive skills (literacy, numeracy, academic achievement tests) can lead to improved opportunities related to tertiary education attendance and labour market outcomes. Improving levels of social and emotional skills (including perseverance, self-esteem and sociability) can lead to improved health-related outcomes and subjective well-being as well as reducing antisocial behaviours. In addition, conscientiousness, sociability and emotional stability are among the important social and emotional skills that also affect children's future prospects.

One of the most significant findings of the OECD report is that social and emotional skills do not act in isolation (OECD 2015). The findings show that the effects of social and emotional skills is realised not only through their direct effects, but additionally through their interactive effects with new learning in cognitive skills (Figure 3.3). That is, 'Skills beget skills' – children with higher levels of social and emotional skills are likely to benefit more from investment to further develop cognitive skills. The implication is that small ability gaps early in life can lead to significant gaps over the life cycle. Therefore, the earlier that children start developing and building a firm foundation for their social emotional skills the greater the opportunity for success across all aspects of their adult life. This highlights the importance of early and continuous investment in social and emotional skill development in the early childhood years for improving future outcomes for children (OECD 2015).

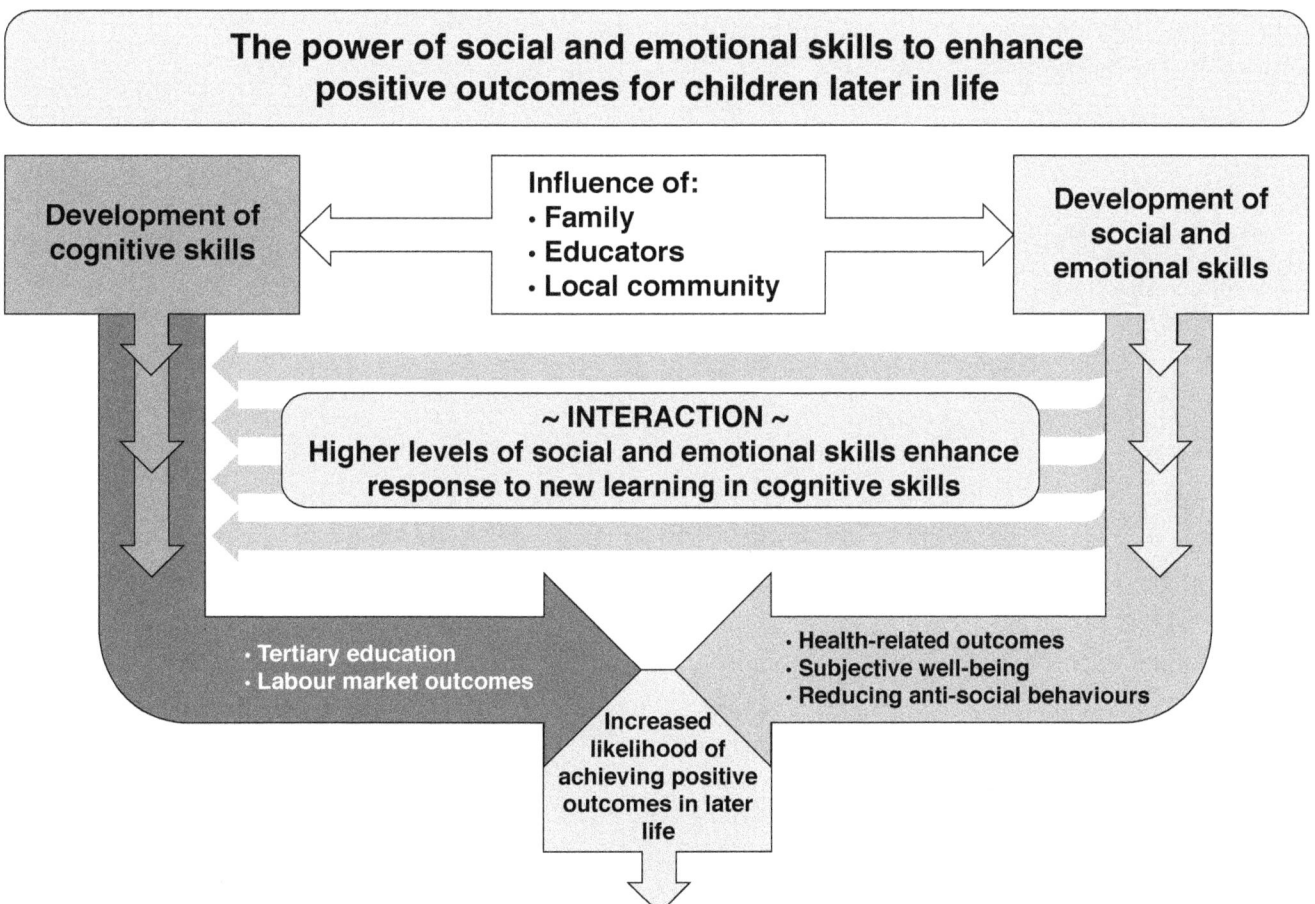

Figure 3.3 The development of social and emotional skills has a significant effect on a child's future prospects. This effect is realised not only directly through these skills but additionally through the interactive effect of social and emotional skills with new learning in cognitive skills. (Adapted from OECD 2015.)

Brain development: uniqueness and diversity

There is a generalised temporal pattern of development for all aspects of growth and development including executive functioning skills; however, this is not a lock step where each child is locked into the same pattern and timing of development. Each individual will have their own pathway that is unique to their own genetic transcript. This is no more apparent than when viewing a group of children of the same age – the diversity in patterns of maturation are evident by observing basic things such as growth in height and difference in physical maturation. While we can see the diversity in rates and patterns of physical maturation, we often forget that a similar diversity would be apparent in children's development in the brain. This is in fact the case, as reported by John Medina (Medina 2012):

- The various regions of the brain develop at different rates in different people.
- No two people's brains store the same information in the same way in the same place.

The implication of these data for all educators is important, but is particularly significant for early childhood educators. Understanding and responding in daily practice to the diversity in brain development and processing is critical to set each child up for success in their own right. The ideal environment for a child to learn is when the child interacts at the 'zone of proximal development' (Vygotsky 1978) – that is, where the child operates at the 'cusp of their learning' (Berk & Winsler 1995). This is where the child 'knows some … but not all', where the child is challenged so they are extended but experience some form of success. It is the prior knowledge that the child uses as the platform for the new learning and the new learning is most successful when the child takes risks, tests, tries new things, fails and self-corrects. This is referred to as a deep learning paradox, where the child (Coyle 2009):

- experiences targeted struggling
- operates at the edge their ability
- make mistakes and corrects.

Given the diversity in brain development and the way an individual brain processes and functions one wonders why educators would ever predominantly work with a whole group instruction model. In early childhood, honouring and respecting each individual and understanding their stage of development is paramount for setting a child up for success. Walker Learning provides a pedagogy that has systems, processes and practice that enable the educator to personalise learning for every child. The starting point to personalising learning is a pedagogy that embeds open-ended play experiences that provide real and rich opportunities to develop social and emotional, academic and executive functioning skills in all children.

Importance of open-ended play experiences

Humans are born with an innate desire to explore, to be inquisitive, to be curious and to ask questions, to learn through a series of self-corrected ideas and failures, to make predictions, to test these predictions and then formulate the next hypothesis to test. This desire to explore is evident in babies. It is during opportunities to play that humans, like all other mammals, learn about life and develop skills for survival. Unfortunately, modern society in its endeavour to set children up for success, is creating an environment that provides the polar opposite of what the developing brain needs most – open-ended play! Play is being superseded by flash cards, DVDs on how to improve children's intelligence, screen time and training time (tennis, ballet, swimming – even for three year olds!). This trend coincides with a reduction of free time available to children: for instance, there was a 25 per cent reduction in children's free time from 1981 to 1997. In 1997 children had an average of 11 hours a week (including screen time) of free time (Medina 2014, p. 131). Many early childhood educators are feeling this 'push down' effect, particularly from parents. Educators often feel they are increasingly under pressure to formally teach children literacy and numeracy. Moreover, there is an emerging trend in early childhood education for children to undertake 'projects/topics' and cloned art work, stencils and cut-outs. These activities are not consistent with what the developing brain needs most – and in many instances these programs are reducing the early childhood experience to a babysitting session rather than rigorous early childhood pedagogy.

Rigorous early childhood education pedagogy is one that embraces the knowledge that open-ended play is as important for the developing brain as protein (Medina 2014). Research has shown comprehensively that children who have engaged in open-ended play (compared to controls) have (Medina 2014):

- enhanced creativity
- more developed oral language
- better problem-solving skills
- lower levels of stress
- stronger memory development
- more developed social skills
- greater impulse control and self-regulation.

This list includes all aspects of executive function skills. There are also additional skills developed across all developmental domains when open-ended play experiences are provided in a wide range of areas: dramatic play, sensory play, construction, collage, painting, carpentry, reading, science and nature.

Dramatic and creative play provides a rich opportunity for children to develop these skills. When a child is engaged in creative dramatic play, neural growth factors are released in the brain. During this engagement a child can practise the skills and behaviours being modelled and scaffolded by adults in their world. In addition, when they are involved in creative play with others they need to think, plan and communicate ideas, negotiate roles, follow rules, react and respond to changes, control their impulses and remember their roles. All these opportunities provide a real and rich opportunity to develop and extend all of their executive functioning skills.

Sensory experiences are also a critical component of any early childhood pedagogy. Sensory experiences provide opportunities for children to be creative, develop fine motor skills, to sooth and to calm. But sensory experiences provide an even more powerful opportunity. This is related to the evolution of the senses working together (e.g. vision influencing hearing), which means that people learn best if several senses are stimulated at once. It is important to stimulate all senses; smell in particular is unusually effective at evoking memory – the evocative smell of old cut lunches often brings us back to the corridors of our own schooling, or the wafting smell of popcorn may provoke recall of 10 to 50 per cent more details of a recent movie. The implication for the educator is that children engaging in multisensory environments always do better than those in uni-sensory environments. Research shows multisensory environments result in more recall with better resolution that lasts longer (evident even 20 years later) (Medina 2014).

Another important component of open-ended play experiences is that a child's competence is not a barrier to successful engagement and experience. Intentional and creative open-ended experiences will provide 'entry points' for children to engage in playing, exploring and learning regardless of their stage of social and emotional development, cognitive or academic skills. In addition, the educator scaffolding the learning through the skill acquisition and process (not end product) not only provides experiences to develop executive function skills but also creates an opportunity for each child to experience success. Chapter 5 provides a summary of the theoretical and practical components of rigorous play pedagogy for early childhood educators.

Contextual experience and then repeat, repeat ... and repeat!

Children learn best when their learning experiences are real, relevant and meaningful, and presented as an experience that is contextual to them and their life. Providing real-life examples, practical experience and hands-on learning are the hallmark attributes to effective early childhood education (OECD 2015). The dramatic play area, for instance, is set up to represent a setting that the children relate to in their own life such as a familiar place they would visit with family and friends (the local cafe, fishing shop, vet clinic, the local hospital).

When these areas are set up with intentional provocations they provide opportunities for perspective taking, and the children engage in hands-on, real-life role play where they develop oral language, social skills, and numeracy and literacy. This conceptual understanding of real, relevant and meaningful experiences is discussed more fully in Chapters 5 and 6.

Contextual experiences are particularly significant when a child is introduced to a new learning or concept; the more the learning is 'contextual' to the child the more consolidated this initial learning will be in the child's memory and cognitive processes (Medina 2014). Once this foundational learning is experienced, children need repeat opportunities to consolidate and extend their thinking and understanding of the new learning. Thus, the ideal learning opportunity is when the first exposure is contextual, and is then followed by repeat opportunities for consolidation and extension through scaffolding from the educator. In addition, a child has an increased chance of remembering the learning if the repeat experiences take place in a similar context or environment (Medina 2012; 2014).

Deep structural learning (when a child goes back to an experience repeatedly) is consistent with the neuroscience data. The contextual experience that is repeated in the same environment is the ideal scenario for a child to embed in their memory. An additional bonus to deep structural learning is that these repeat experiences provide the ideal conduit for the development of oral language – where the child has repeat conversations about the same thing with an adult. These data highlight the need for open-ended play experiences that are set up intentionally and creatively by the educator, and where the educator extends the child's thinking and experiences through provocations, scaffolding and modelling.

Relationships, relationships, relationships: face time

Humans need and desire to form relationships and to relate to others. For a child, relationships and attachment have significant influence on the wiring of their brain – their learning, their emotional state, the development of self-concept and the development of executive function. The importance of secure attachment for long-term emotional stability, self-concept and the development of executive function has been well documented. Moreover, it has been demonstrated in recent research that strong relationships between educators and children is one of the critical determinants of successful early childhood education (Melhuish 2015; OECD 2015). However, despite the compelling data related to the negative outcomes of insecure attachments, there is evidence of an increase in insecure attachments in affluent Western societies (Manne 2014). The main culprits being tagged are the outsourcing of parenting, children being given mixed messages, a chaotic home life with inconsistent or absent primary carers and absent parents who compensate by overindulging their children in materialistic rewards, alongside an emphasis on achievement through winning rather than encouraging the child's efforts and attempts.

In this modern-day context the importance of relationships with early childhood educators and children becomes paramount. In contrast, however, too often relationships with children is at the lower end of the list (if on the list at all), with priority being given to taking a multitude of photos, observations at a distance and excessive irrelevant documentation. The end result is that educators have very little time or inclination to be in a moment of mindfulness with a child, to deepen their relationship with a child, or to authentically know and understand the child.

The importance of attachment and relationships with children is highlighted by the evidence that the stronger the attachment a child has to an educator the more likely they are to take a risk in their learning, the more likely they will transition through difficult times at home, and the more likely the educator will pitch it just right for the child. Building relationships and attachment does not just happen; it is not an automatic consequence of the educator just being around.

Building relationships with a child takes time (authentic time with the child), takes skill from the educator, requires empathy from the educator and needs the educator to honour the child for who they are. The educator demonstrating empathy with the child is the foundation of effective development of resonance and attachments (Medina 2014).

Despite attachment and relationships being the cornerstone of early child education, and absurd though it may seem, very few educators have participated in professional learning about how to deepen their relationships with children or how to develop an empathy response for children. Chapter 4 on communication and relationships provides an introduction to the emotional intelligence model related to building and strengthening relationships with children.

In addition to the development of attachment, authentic time spent with a child provides an important opportunity for the development of non-verbal communication – looking at them, and sharing gestures with consistent oral communication is critical for the child to develop their understanding of emotional information (see Figure 3.4). Relationships depend on interpreting non-verbal communication and to cross-check this with verbal communication. The development of this skill starts almost as soon as a baby is born and develops over many years. That is why babies and young children need human time in their earliest years – interaction with parent and educator on a consistent basis.

Figure 3.4 In addition to the development of attachment, authentic time spent with a child provides an important opportunity for the development of non-verbal communication. Looking at them, and sharing gestures with consistent oral communication, is critical for the child to develop their understanding of emotional information.

The modelling of the educator also provides a powerful learning experience for the child. Deferred imitation is where the child has the ability to reproduce behaviour after witnessing the event only once. A 13 month old can remember an event a week after a single exposure and an 18 month old can recall an event and reproduce the behaviour after four months from the single exposure. Any educator working in dramatic play would have witnessed children's sophisticated capacity for deferred imitation (particularly in the home corner!). Relationships, empathy and modelling appropriate behaviour are all significant components of early childhood education and require knowledge, skill and intention from the educator. It takes even greater skill and understanding from the educator to respond with empathy for a child who does not have the skills to function in the environment and has been labelled 'bad' or 'naughty'. As noted earlier in this chapter, a child who has difficulties with self-regulation is likely to have very challenging behaviour and require more time and understanding from the educator – not less. Early childhood educators need to provide an environment of consistency, predictability and stability for all children and in particular the children who are most needy. The challenging children are generally the most needy, and what they need most is a stable educator who is patient, calming, accepting and consistent; not one who makes judgments of behaviour, but instead asks – I wonder why? Chapter 4 on relationships provides educators with information on understanding and skills to deepen their relationships with children.

Implications of developmental neuroscience for early childhood pedagogy

The implications of developmental neuroscience in practice in early childhood education include:

- short attention spans – so short group times
- babies rooms and toddlers rooms not looking the same as three- and four-year-old rooms
- spaces not dominated by tables
- cosy corners used to define spaces
- giving children the opportunity to return to experiences, to play repeatedly in the same way; for the educator to scaffold, extend and have repeat conversations with children within the same play space
- invitational group times; not making all children participate in group time
- deinstitutionalising the early childhood setting – it is not a rehearsal for school
- open-ended experiences – not activities and not stencilled or cloned experiences
- smiling, wise and consistent educators for relationships and attachment for the child
- same educators following children through levels for building attachment and relationships.

Summary

The key aims of this chapter are to show that:

- using evidence as a basis for practice moves early childhood education into a deeper and more professional standard of education

- drawing upon recent research about neurology and biology can complement family, culture and environmental considerations

- ensuring all educators have and acquire knowledge so that evidence is used for decision making in everyday practice is an imperative; otherwise, personal inclination dominates and decisions are made on the run.

Suggested resources

Akbari, E & McCuaig, K 2014, *Early Childhood Education Report 2014*, Ontario Institute for Studies in Education, Toronto.

Center on the Developing Child 2011, *Building the brain's 'air traffic control' system: how early experiences shape the development of executive function*, Working paper 11, Harvard University, Cambridge, MA.

Medina, J 2012, *Brain rules: 12 principles for surviving and thriving at work, home and school*, Scribe, Brunswick, Victoria.

Medina, J 2014, *Brain rules for baby. How to raise a smart and happy child from zero to five*, Scribe, Brunswick, Victoria.

OECD 2015, 'Skills for social progress: the power of social and emotional skills', in OECD Skills Studies series (ed.), OECD, Paris.

Chapter 4
Communication and relationships with children, colleagues and parents

'The most important thing in communication is hearing what isn't being said.'

Peter Drucker

Introduction

The human brain is wired for relationships and attachment; as a species, humans would not survive without attachment and bonds with others. Relationships and interactions between significant adults and babies and young children are critical for the facilitation of brain development, future relationships, physical growth, language acquisition, pro-social behaviours and to significantly facilitate positive adult mental health and psychological well-being. Supportive relationships that promote healthy attachment improve children's understanding and regulation of emotions as well as their feelings of security and motivation for exploration and learning (OECD 2015). The scientific basis for these crucial interactions has been discussed in depth in the previous chapter on neuroscience (Chapter 3).

The foundation for best practice in early childhood education is defined by the importance of relationships, effective communication and interactions. Longitudinal research from the United Kingdom reports that high-quality early childhood education has a significant difference on long-term positive outcomes in life when compared to poorer-quality preschool education. The characteristics that defined high-quality compared with low-quality education were the interactions and relationships between the educators and the children (Melhuish 2015; Sylva et al. 2004).

Relationships with children are the foundation of Walker Learning pedagogy, as is the case for the majority of early childhood theories and philosophies around the world. Yet, despite the powerful evidence supporting the importance of adult relationships and interactions for babies and young children there is an incomprehensible absence of this training or even acknowledgment of it in most education university degrees and diplomas. Rarely do early childhood education students have the opportunity to develop their understanding and skills in effective communication, self-awareness in working with children, how to explicitly build relationships with children, and how to respond to children at a deep emotional and psychological level. This situation is made even worse by some training facilities offering very simplistic behaviour management processes of extrinsic motivation such as rewards and bribes (e.g. star charts and stickers), or punishment and humiliation (e.g. naughty corner). The early childhood years are the most critical years of development that influence an individual's future life and as a profession it is our duty of care to use evidence-based practice to ensure optimal opportunities for all children. When children trust through relationships, they are more likely to:

- bounce back
- have a go
- take a risk
- behave
- be intrinsically motivated
- feel emotionally safe
- develop independence and interdependence
- learn and acquire skill and understandings
- build new relationships
- pattern the brain for future relationships throughout their lifetime.

In this chapter we present an introduction to an emotional intelligence model to facilitate relationships and communication with children. The emotional intelligence model, based on neuroscience research and Walker Learning, embeds emotional intelligence (EI) throughout the pedagogy. Being more emotionally intelligent is a lifelong journey and this chapter presents the very beginning of this journey. The latter part of the chapter is dedicated to guiding educators to be proactive (rather than reactive) in their relationships and communications with children. We hope you enjoy reading this chapter, but more importantly we hope it is an ignition point for your continued journey in self-development and commitment to working with young children.

Emotional intelligence model of building relationships

Introduction to emotional intelligence

Decades of research have shown that the only consistent predictor of adult happiness is a person's relationships to other people. This means that friendships are a better predictor of happiness than any other single factor, and interestingly the two strongest predictors for social competency (e.g. ability to form friendships) *are emotional regulation* and *empathic understanding* (Medina 2014). It is no surprise therefore that these two components are two major pillars of emotional intelligence. An emotional intelligence model for building relationships is based on our understanding of the science of the brain. While the intelligence quotient (IQ) has traditionally been used to identify certain characteristics of a person's intelligence, an IQ has significant limitations in identifying a person's ability and capacity for social competence, communication and interpersonal relationships. In contrast, the basis of emotional intelligence is all about being emotionally smart, or emotionally intelligent, and refers to the ability to use one's emotions in a smart and intuitive way (Feldman & Mulle 2007). Emotional intelligence provides a model whereby we learn to become more aware of ourselves, which then puts us in a much more empowered position to be able to manage emotions more effectively.

The emotional intelligence model makes the following two assumptions:

1. What we do, and what we teach we can almost take for granted. This is, we are employed as early childhood educators because we have a degree and/or expertise in early childhood education.
2. How we do it and who we are as we do it, is what makes some of us exceptional and inspiring in our relationships with children. That is, having a degree in early childhood education does not necessarily imply that we will be effective or inspirational as an educator for children.

In the emotional intelligence model, building *resonance* with others is the key strategy for developing relationships. Resonance with another can be best described by some of the following common statements:

- 'I just feel on the same wavelength …'
- 'We just clicked …'
- 'It felt so natural, we got on so easily.'

These feelings with another person are more than an 'airy fairy' form of clicking, but are actually the result of a chemical reaction in the brain when two people 'connect' or build resonance. The more one connects with another the greater the resonance and the deeper the relationship. For children, the greater resonance the educator builds with the child the stronger the attachment the child has to the educator and the stronger the relationship.

It is easy (almost automatic) to develop resonance with people who we feel are similar to us; however, it takes an active intentional process and practise to build resonance with individuals who are not so similar. This is the skill of an emotionally intelligent educator – one who is able to develop resonance with children, colleagues or parents who may not necessarily be similar or easily connected with. The skill and active process of building resonance comes from the educator being able to exhibit an empathy response for the other.

An empathy response is a cognitive process where one can actually understand someone else's perspective. Empathy does not require a solution – it only requires understanding. Reflective listening is a key strategy that educators can use to create empathy with the child. This is discussed later in this chapter. Choosing to empathise with children is so powerful it can change the developing nervous systems of infants if practised regularly (Medina 2014). In fact, empathy not only matters; it is the foundation of effective communication for children by primary adults in their life. An empathy response is very different to showing 'sympathy'. Sympathy is where one emotionally feels for the other and is often caught up in that feeling.

In summary, empathy is a cognitive process that enables the understanding of the perspective of the other and is not about problem solving. Sympathy on the other hand is an emotional response that lacks cognitive understanding of the perspective of the other – it is about feeling the emotion. In most instances in early childhood education the aim is for educators to exhibit an empathy response. Of course, there will be times when sympathy may be needed, but in the majority of cases the child needs the adult to empathise with them. This core concept underpins emotional intelligence, Walker Learning and the proactive strategies presented in the latter half of the chapter.

Emotional intelligence works from a four-component model for successful communication, building relationships and working with others. The starting point for many is to try to manage others (including managing children!). We often think, 'If only "they" would change', or 'If only "they" would do it differently'. In contrast the emotionally intelligent individual will start at the other end of the spectrum; this means aiming to understand one's self as the first priority in relationship building. Being emotionally intelligent is shown in Figure 4.1.

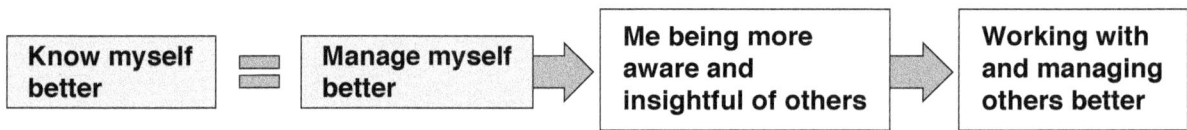

Figure 4.1 The emotional intelligence model is based on the following sequence for relationship building and communication: The more I know myself, the more I can manage myself. The more I can manage myself, the more I understand others and the more I understand others, the more I am effectively able to manage them, rather than think I have to change them. (Adapted from Feldman & Mulle 2007, pp. 11–12.)

Emotionally intelligent people accept that there is little (if anything) they can do to change others directly, but they can, in knowing themselves, become more effective at accepting others, being open to others, and being a role model for others. They also understand that creating resonance for others builds trust, thus allowing them to express how they feel and to feel more emotionally secure, and creates inspiration, gives empathy (but not necessarily sympathy) and brings from within them a positivity that is often infectious.

A person who is developing emotionally intelligent elements as they interact with others is likely to demonstrate the following characteristics:

- displays a bright, upbeat mood
- has an injection of humour
- ensures positive and direct eye contact
- is conscious and aware of persona/body language
- presents a positive perspective in the first instance
- reflects empathy rather than sympathy
- uses self as a model for desired interactions
- is inclusive and talks up the 'collective', 'we', 'us'
- smiles!

This doesn't happen overnight, but we can start straightaway and don't need deep therapy to make it happen. We just start practising consciously and let emotionally intelligent elements become part of our new pattern of behaviour. The more we change, the more impact we have upon others.

The following sections provide a brief overview of the four elements of building emotional intelligence skills from the perspective of early childhood education: knowing one's self, managing one's self, knowing others (e.g. child/parent/colleague) and managing and guiding others (e.g. child/parent/colleague).

Knowing one's self

The greatest way to work effectively with children is to have intuitive and responsive educators, and the first step to achieving this is for the educators to know themselves well. Some of the most powerful questions we can ask ourselves as educators when working with children include:

- How well do I know myself?
- Am I self-aware?
- Have I ever considered how I was parented?
- What changes may I need to make about myself?

- What do I do and how do I respond without thinking?
- Am I too moralistic?
- Do I respond to children without really thinking and simply replay my own communication experiences with my parents?
- Do I bring my own values into the learning environment that may or may not be appropriate?
- Do I allow children to express their feelings?
- Do I force them to say sorry even when they don't feel sorry? Am I therefore teaching them to lie and not be honest about their feelings?
- Do I force them to 'Put on their happy face' when they actually feel sad?
- Do I work hard to build a meaningful relationship with children?

The above questions are just the tip of the iceberg in relation to how all communication and interactions with children start, with the adult taking responsibility. First is knowing yourself and making the effort to intentionally develop a deeper understanding of who you are as a person and as an educator. The following is a list of aspects of self-awareness that is a useful tool for all educators to use as opportunities to self-reflect. The self-aware educator:

- is aware of their own emotions and reactions
- clearly expresses feelings
- is intuitive
- presents as intellectually capable
- is aware of their own strengths and weaknesses
- is open to feedback from others
- possesses confidence in their own abilities
- is critically reflective about situations and decisions
- learns from their own experiences and those of others
- seeks opportunities for self-development.

Another aspect of understanding yourself is related to temperament; the innate traits that represent who you are as a person. Temperament is often referred to as your personality. There is a section on temperament later in the chapter when we discuss the 'goodness of fit' proactive strategy for educators to use when working with children.

Managing one's self

While understanding self is the very important first step in the emotional intelligence model it is the next step (managing self) that sets the educator up to be in a more mindful and open position to understand a child and to ultimately work successfully with the child. As we discussed in Chapter 3, self-regulation is a very important executive function skill for success in life, and as we have read earlier in this chapter, self-regulation is a key characteristics to facilitating friendship groups ... which is the key to happiness!

Managing self sometimes is easy and at other times very challenging; in any case, the first step is to be aware about the need to self-manage, to take responsibility for your actions and to understand how to manage yourself to create the best outcome for children. The second step is to practise managing self; the more you practise the more likely you will be able to manage yourself in the more challenging situations.

Managing yourself as an educator requires you to reflect on how you respond to different situations with children – to identify your default position. A person's default position is related to the attitudes and behaviours that have become embedded over the course of their life and hence are the first response in a situation. Self-management needs to be strong and present if a person's default position is incongruent with best practice of working with children. An example that demonstrates this is to first ask yourself what are the needs and challenges of children that you find difficult as an educator, and then reflect on what your default position would be related to your response. You could generally respond with:

- a knee-jerk reaction (e.g. I think to myself 'I have to stop that behaviour')

- being judgmental (that child is just attention seeking)
- anxiousness (I wonder what I should do and I hope it won't upset anyone)
- being reflective (I wonder what is causing that behaviour? I wonder why?).

In terms of working with colleagues and parents, these are the characteristics that describe self-management in the emotional intelligence model. The self-managing educator is one who:

- is ethically responsible
- presents with self-assurance
- displays emotional self-control and emotional resilience
- is motivated
- is conscientious
- is willing to make a hard decision when necessary
- is professionally committed
- is honest and transparent in interactions with others.

Walker Learning places relationships as one of its major platforms, and self-awareness and self-management as the means to effectively build relationships and effective communication with children. The attribution of managing self underpins the understanding that it is the educator's responsibility to manage themselves, not the child's responsibility to be like an adult.

Knowing the child (social awareness and understanding)

Knowing a child from a holistic perspective is a hallmark of Walker Learning and is related to the third quadrant of the emotional intelligence model. Knowing a child from a holistic perspective relates to the child's family, history, culture, religion, health, strength, challenges, temperament and development. Knowing the child in a deeper, more meaningful way facilitates the opportunity for the educator to get it just right for that individual child. One size fits all is the antithesis of early childhood education and the more we understand the child the more we are able to guide and work with the child effectively as an individual and so improve the chance of success for the child.

In addition to understanding each child, there are also developmental understandings of the early childhood years that inform our understanding of children. The early childhood years are characterised as:

- a time for testing limits
- a time for pushing boundaries
- a time for questioning
- a time for anxieties
- a time for limited understandings
- a time for early identity formation.

The child at this time often:

- is egocentric
- has limited concentration
- is exploratory
- is not always able to articulate their emotions
- is socially and emotionally still maturing
- is easily shamed
- has difficulty in regulating their emotions.

The educator needs to keep these understandings of development in the early childhood years at the forefront of their thinking with all interactions with children.

In terms of working with colleagues and parents, the key characteristics of an educator who has social awareness and understanding from an emotionally intelligent perspective include:

- manages staff/team relationships well
- uses humour
- displays interpersonal sensitivity
- is empathetic
- demonstrates perspective taking
- accurately assesses the feelings and needs of others
- displays cultural sensitivity

- supports team building
- influences – inspires, motivates, engenders a spirit of willing cooperation
- is discerning.

The next section is related to working and guiding children (relationship management).

Working and guiding the child (relationship management)

The emotional intelligence model proposes that when the educator is self-aware, manages their self well and has a deep understanding of the child, then they are in a position to be proactive with their guidance and education of the child. The most powerful way of responding to children, and working with and interpreting children's needs and behaviours is to have adults who are:

- reflective
- open to change
- open to critical analysis
- committed to viewing the child first and the child's behaviour second.

As discussed in the section above on understanding the child, we know that just children being children presents challenges for the early childhood educator. For some children, some challenges may be more intense and more prolonged than others, and this is particularly the case for children who have experienced trauma and/or have delayed or compromised executive functioning skills. With these children in particular it is the adult who needs to work mostly on themselves, rather than on the challenging behaviours of the child. Change takes time and there are no quick fixes in helping children develop positive behaviours. All behaviour has meaning behind it and it is up to the adult to ensure they understand, interpret and respond to the meaning. We hear adults stating in response to a child's inappropriate behaviours, 'Just ignore them, they are just attention seeking'. As an example, a child may be hitting and swearing, but a mindful educator will look beyond the behaviour and ask 'I wonder why?' There are numerous reasons why a child may be hitting and swearing – it may be because there is domestic violence/abuse at home, it may be because the child is delayed in development and is finding the experiences frustrating, it may be because the child is copying the behaviour of other children, or it may be due to something else. Clearly the motivation behind the behaviour needs to be understood so that the educator can respond to the child in a mindful and purposeful way, and not with a knee-jerk reaction. In Walker Learning we view 'equity as difference' – that is, to provide equity to all children we need to provide difference to meet the needs of each individual child.

It is obvious that if a child is behaving inappropriately and using attention-seeking behaviours then they are in need of attention and that something is wrong! Children do not wake up in the morning at the ripe old age of three years and plan ahead and decide at what time of the day at their centre they will start to misbehave. We all know that the child who has some level of trust, despite how challenging their behaviours are, is most likely to respond at some level. The key to working with all children, regardless of whether or not they have an obvious need or challenging behaviours is to understand that all children are prewired for meaningful relationships and it is imperative that these are proactively built and progressed by a self-aware, self-managing, reflective adult.

In these times of challenge, educators need to remind themselves that:

- children are not born bad
- children are not just wanting attention or being manipulative to make the educator's life hard
- children and adults form habits of behaviours based upon experiences, learning difficulties, stress, family disturbance and low self-esteem.

To work and guide children in a proactive way educators need to view behaviour as a way of informing understanding. Reflection on a child's behaviour and the meaning behind this behaviour is captured in the following:

- Behaviour is always a communication between child and adult – the most important thing in communication is to hear what isn't being said (Neven 1996).
- Behaviour stems from unconscious or conscious motivations or dilemmas.

- Behaviour is dynamic and changes all the time, and it changes over time between adults and children.
- The emotionally intelligent educator reflects and ponders: 'What might it mean for the child?' and, 'I wonder why'.

We don't want to just fix or manage their behaviours, we want to respond to the motivations and needs behind their behaviours. If a child is attention seeking, then it is obvious something needs attention! Instead of a knee-jerk reaction, judging or an anxiety-based reaction, a reflective educator may consider and reflect on how they are feeling and responding to the child and the circumstance (this is examined later in this chapter).

In terms of working with colleagues and parents the key characteristics of an educator who is able to develop relationships from an emotionally intelligent perspective include:

- fosters bonds between team members
- establishes effective relationships with others
- maintains a wide network of contacts
- is supportive and encouraging
- openly shares information with others
- seeks feedback
- displays listening skills
- acknowledges and celebrates the success of others.

The following section describes proactive strategies the educator can use to be in a more empowered position to work and guide children in a positive way.

Proactive strategies to guide children's behaviour and build relationships

The more proactive an educator can be with their interactions with children the greater the chance is of building trust, for the child to transition through difficult times and for the child to build their skills and understandings. Too often overworked educators do not have the time or understanding to be proactive with their interactions and end up being in a constant state of reactivity. When the educator is in this constant state of reactivity, there is no time or space to consider the child or what is driving the child's behaviour. Being in a state of reactivity is the opposite to being in a state of mindfulness. Without being calm, mindful and respectful of the child there is limited opportunity to build trust, relationships or attachment.

We have to be proactive, not just reactive!

Building trust, attachment and relationships

Relationships are the fundamental element of what it means to be human: not photographs of children, but being with the children; not a narrative written up about a child, but an authentic conversation with a child; and not a project on snails with a child, but being in the moment with the child in their exploration and sharing the joy and wonder.

Relationships are precious throughout our lives. Walker Learning places relationships first and foremost and considers them to be the work of best practice and evidence-based practice.

Relationships must come before routines, before portfolios and learning stories and documentation. Relationships are what we work on most. Relationships and primary carers are critical for the brain development and emotional development of babies and toddlers. Relationships motivate, inspire, and build trust and care and commitment. Relationships help us all grow throughout our lifetime and, as the ancient Greek philosopher Plato said, 'the beginning is the most important part of any work, especially when it is young and needs time to grow'.

Children need significant adults when they are young, they need these adults to smile, to reflect, to take time, to take care, to nurture, to take it easy, to laugh, to play and to be.

Figure 4.2 Children need you when they are young ... and they need you to be in a state of mindfulness, to be authentically and respectfully in the moment with who they are and where they are.

In building relationships that are meaningful and intuitive, educators need to be able to hold the emotions of children on their behalf, rather than to dismiss them. Children have limited verbal capacity to express clearly and with maturity their own emotions, so reflecting their emotions for them does justice to how they feel. Not being able to express how they feel often leads to children feeling frustrated and upset or unheard.

Important to building trust and attachment is the notion of containment; the adult needs to be capable of 'holding' what the child produces, whether it be crying, biting, hitting, anxiety, anger or discomfort. The adult needs to be able to transform these communications of the child. 'Holding' is the emotional holding of an experience rather than blaming. The education environment also contributes to building trust and relationships by providing the following characteristics:

- appropriate expectations
- relaxing and calm
- empowering/ownership
- consistent
- flexible and adaptive
- not publically shaming.

Proactive communication strategies

There are some key elements in building a repertoire of effective communication interactions with young children. They include:

- reflective listening
- 'I' messages
- temperament: goodness of fit.

Reflective listening

Reflective listening, or active listening as it sometimes referred to, is simply acknowledging and stating back what emotion or issue you think is happening for someone at any given time. Reflective listening is the key strategy for educators to develop resonance with children.

Between adults, for example, it may be that someone has just lost their job. Reflective listening might mean our response upon being told this by the person who was visibly upset is, 'I can see you are very upset about this'. You may then offer support and hold further conversations. In reflective listening, the most important part is often the bit we don't use. We tend to rush into offering support, looking on the bright side, trying to offer alternatives. None of that is wrong and may in fact be appropriate, but the acknowledgment of how someone must be feeling at this point is the critical part of the whole conversation.

One good way to remember how to use reflective listening is to start with an 'I' message or 'It seems that you are ...'. For example,

- 'I can see you are very angry about this'
- 'I can see you are feeling upset about this'.

It may sound a bit contrived to start with, but over time, this becomes a real skill that feels more and more natural. Remember, reflective listening will not fix the problem. Neither is it likely that the person you are talking with who is angry or upset will make a miraculous recovery or thank you for acknowledging how they feel. Reflective listening is not a 'fixing up' technique. It is simply a respectful strategy in helping others to feel that their emotions or experiences are recognised. One of the greatest challenges with people we care about is to accept their feelings and acknowledge them without feeling we have to 'fix them' immediately.

It is important to remember that one of the aims of education and building relationships is to help a child develop the skills and strategies that will enable them to express their needs, wants, feelings and hopes in appropriate ways. We want our young children to develop patterns of communication and healthy self-expression early in life.

'I' messages: owning your own stuff

In communicating with children, we need to take responsibility for our feelings and not make children feel that our emotions are their responsibility, or that they caused us to feel particular ways.

We need to ensure we avoid comments or questions such as the following:

- 'When you do that you make me feel sad.'
- 'Do you want to give me a smile now? I'll feel happy if you do.'
- 'I feel very proud of you.'
- 'How would you like it if that happened to you?'
- 'You wouldn't like it would you if that happened to you?'
- 'We are all friends here.'
- 'You make me feel much better when you smile and share with everyone.'
- 'That's not very nice.'
- 'You say sorry now so they know you didn't mean it.'
- 'Give each other a cuddle so you can be friends again and say sorry.'
- 'Put on your happy face now.'
- 'Be brave.'
- 'You're a big girl now, big girls don't have to cry.'
- 'You show mummy how you don't cry anymore and aren't sad anymore when she leaves.'
- 'You're a big strong boy. Boys are brave.'

All of the above statements and questions make huge assumptions, place demands upon children, reflect non-intuitive adults who are simply parroting things that don't allow children to feel how they may really be feeling. These statements reflect more about what the adults are wanting or expecting the children to do for the adult, rather than what the adult can do for the child.

> *The relationship should not be about what the child can do for the adult but what the adult can do for the child.*

For example, when a parent is leaving a child who is struggling with separation anxiety and the parent says to the child, 'Give Mummy a smile, show mummy you don't cry anymore', this is more for the mother's sake, not the child's. In addition, it fails to acknowledge that the child may be having real emotional difficulty with the separation. It also assumes that the child is able to control their emotions and that life is about control rather than being able to feel, to be nurtured and comforted.

When an adult says 'I'm proud of you', it reflects a misunderstanding that, while it may be intended as an affirmation, it is not the place of someone else (parent or educator) to say or infer how they may feel about a child's own achievement. That is actually up to the child.

When an adult asks a young egocentric child who has not yet developed empathetic cognition (e.g. the ability to understand the perspective and feelings of another) they consequently find it difficult to truly place themselves in the position of another's feelings or thoughts. This is perplexing and confusing, and places the child in a no-win situation if they are expected to understand.

What adults could say in response to the range of emotions of children include the following:

- 'I can see you are feeling sad at the moment.'
- 'I know it is hard when Daddy has to leave.'
- 'I know you were feeling very cross when you hit …'
- 'I know you don't want to pack away the blocks.'
- 'Would you like me to stay with you for a while longer?'
- 'Do you need me to look after you?'
- 'How do you feel about that?'
- 'It's okay to cry if you are feeling sad or missing Mum.'
- 'I can see you have worked hard on that today …'
- 'You don't have to be brave if it is hurting you …'
- 'You seem very frustrated about this …'
- 'I know you don't want to play with him right now, let's find something else to do.'
- 'We don't all have to be friends, but we do have to try not to hurt each other.'

Temperament: goodness of fit

In considering our interactions and relationships, we want to maximise the possibilities of building healthy and positive relationships with everyone. Understanding a bit about our own personality and the personalities of others helps us to make a good fit between ourselves and another.

Making this 'goodness of fit', as it is known, requires us to consider our personality and then consider the personality of each of the children we work with. While we cannot change our general disposition or our personality, we can modify how our personality manifests itself in behaviours and interactions with others.

Consider the following three major personalities:

1. intense
2. slow to warm up
3. easy.

None of them are bad; each has positive and challenging aspects to them.

When we are *intense*, we feel things 'intensely' and our reactions are usually quite full on. You can imagine what that must be like for a young child, who emotionally has difficulty even at the best of times in regulating themselves.

Slow-to-warm-up children are often incorrectly labelled 'shy' or 'reserved'. They often take a little longer to transition from one year level to another, to get used to another group or educator. They find new things or people a bit harder to get used to in the first instant. They need time to 'warm up'; then they are fine.

Easy personalities are not always the easiest! They can be overlooked in a group, they can perhaps be non-demanding, take the easy way out and used as examples for others, all of which can become a burden over time.

Researchers Thomas and Chess suggest that approximately 12 per cent of the population has an intense personality (Chess & Thomas 1984; Thomas & Chess 1977). About 25 per cent has a slow-to-warm-up personality and about 30 per cent has an easy personality. The remainder was too hard to define due to many variables.

The key message here is that in building meaningful relationships with children, it is the adult, *not* the child, who has to make the good fit. It is the adult who reflects and says something like this, 'Gee, I have a tendency to be "intense". That child seems quite intense too. Given they are only two years of age, it will have to be me that calms myself a little. I will need to be a little less intense, so that between me and that child, we have a calmer relationship and I can make a good fit for the child.'

A child not engaged?

Is it me? Is it the child? Is it the environment?

In building relationships with children and considering when aspects of the relationship or behaviours and interactions are not working well, the adult needs to be capable, open and reflective enough to consider some key questions:

- Is it me?
- Is it the child?
- Is it the expectations in and of the environment itself?

Let us consider these three pivotal questions of reflection.

1. Is it me?
- Am I open to this child?
- Am I judging this child and family?
- Am I blaming the child?
- Do I not seem to actually like this child?
- Am I being impatient?
- Am I rushing this child?
- Do I not like the child's parents?
- Do I find the child confronting?
- Do I hear myself thinking the child is just attention seeking?
- Do I need to work harder in building this relationship?
- Do I not understand this child and why they are doing or not doing something?
- Do I feel threatened by this child's behaviour or words?
- Does this child trigger a emotional response in me from somewhere?
- Is this a new experience for me and do I feel like I'm not coping?
- Am I feeling under pressure?
- Am I feeling like a failure with this child?
- Are there other's expectations upon me with this child?

2. Is it the child?
- Does the child need a primary attachment figure?
- Does the child have a difficult or challenging family life?
- Is the child fearful?
- Can the child understand me?
- Is the child immature emotionally?
- Is there a developmental delay or other possible neurological or medical issue?
- Does the child have a possible hearing issue?
- Is the child teething?
- What is the child's prior and current context?
- What appears to be the child's need?
- What are the things the child responds to?

3. Is it the expectations in and of the environment itself?
- Is the environment under- or over-stimulating?

- Is the environment too noisy and busy?
- Do we force the child to come to group time when they are just not ready yet?
- Do we make the child lie down or try to sleep, causing distress?
- Are we calm enough?
- Do we provide enough real choice and flexibility?
- Do we provide a rich range of cosy corners; for example, hideaway spaces, sensory and tactile areas for soothing?
- Are our routines predictable but relaxed and calm?
- Are the experiences open-ended?
- Are there experiences intentionally planned to be engaging for this child?

A centre philosophy and strategies

In early childhood, developing and maintaining relationships between educators and children requires deep thinking and strategies at a number of levels. At an infrastructure level, many centres are now considering or implementing family groupings throughout the entire day.

This means that children are able to be with their siblings. This is significant because being part of the family structure is very important for young children. It also means that the educators working with the group follow the group over a number of years, maximising relationships with families and the children. It is very artificial and difficult for young children who finally attach with an adult to have to lose that attachment figure just because they have a birthday or because there is no room left in a particular room. Relationships and sustaining meaningful relationships between key adults and children is of paramount importance.

It is also not ideal developmentally, or even natural, to have many children of the same age and stage of maturity all in the same room for many hours each day, all with similar and competing needs. Some centres, while still having children of similar ages in the same room, have the educators follow the children through each year so the children are able to sustain their primary carers and the staff maximise their relationships with the children.

It is time in early childhood that we really re-examine and revisit how we group children and assign educators. So many young children, particularly under the age of three are put through extremely upsetting scenarios because the system expects things of them that their emotional and psychological development is not designed for them to have to cope with. While there has been much debate related to ratios of children per adult, there has been an absence of conversation around relationships, attachment and grouping of children.

How do we as adults, as educators, as a profession, ensure that as many educators as possible do have the ability to reflect, to be open to change and to know themselves well so that relationships and responses to children are at a very high level? The personal work of becoming self-aware and managing ourselves is the approach that can achieve this.

None of us are able to claim that we are already 'naturals' at working effectively with children, or that none of us have work to do on knowing ourselves, our motivations, our reactions, our personalities, our values, our own childhoods and how we were parented, our own internal motivations and emotional triggers or responses. The greatest communicators and the most meaningful relationships in any aspect of our lives are when we know ourselves well and we think and consciously work hard at how we live our relationships.

Working proactively with colleagues and parents

Each educator should pursue their own personal growth towards understanding themselves in order to manage themselves to maximise their relationships. Educators need to work towards understanding children more deeply and responding more authentically and appropriately, both to the children and the adults in their personal and professional lives. As educators we work not only with children but also with their parents, families and with a range of other professionals.

It is often discussed in centres that working with the children is the easy bit and working with the parents is the more challenging aspect. We also know that having to work so closely alongside our team members takes an enormous amount of effort in order to work well for our sakes and particularly for the children's sakes.

Conflict can occur between educators and this, despite everyone's best efforts, always creates tension in the learning environment.

Effective communication and productive workplace relationships are not about friendship, but rather about professional and effective highly reflective practitioners, who work hard to understand themselves so that they can manage themselves first in order to understand the others they work with.

Being able to communicate using 'I' messages and being able to honestly say to someone, 'I am having trouble understanding what we are doing', rather than talking behind their back about how you don't like what they are doing, makes a more relaxed and open workplace. Being able to assert how you feel, being able to reflect upon what you might need to change rather than blaming everyone else, and being able to think deeply to consider what might be happening for the other person, to be intuitive and articulate, are the elements of communication and relationships that need to be worked on and honoured in the workplace.

An emotionally intelligent educator also knows when the workplace is not healthy to be in, or when it is time to move on because the environment does not provide the safety or security in which workers can communicate openly or reflect and grow. In the end, such a decision needs to come from reflecting on what is right and what is the duty of care to the children.

Summary

The key aims of this chapter are to show that:

- relationships are the foundation for work with children
- knowing ourselves and being able to reflect upon our reactions and responses, and to manage ourselves and our behaviour, is one of the most important elements of our professional life
- using an emotional intelligence framework empowers us to become more emotionally self-aware and more effective at managing ourselves so as to facilitate optimal opportunities for children, parents and colleagues
- viewing the child and their behaviour as an expression of need or communication rather than simply as attention seeking or naughty enables us to consider more deeply our responses to support the child.

Suggested resource

Feldman, J & Mulle, K 2007, *Put emotional intelligence to work*, American Society of Training and Development, Alexandria, Virginia.

Chapter 5

Overview of play from a teaching and learning perspective

'The true sign of intelligence is not knowledge but imagination.'

Albert Einstein

Introduction

One of the most important aspects of our work in early childhood education is to educate children: 'to educate' means that children learn, develop and acquire skills, concepts and understandings. In addition to this core understanding of education Walker Learning embraces the notion of educating the 'whole child', including not only the emotional and social, cognitive, language and physical aspects of a child's development, but factoring in their neurological, genetically based predisposition to personality, their literacy and numeracy, the arts and, of course, their cultures, family and the wider political and environmental influences that impact upon the biological elements of development.

The commitment to the whole child requires rigorous planning and documentation; it requires high levels of intention and it requires a high degree of scaffolding from the educator in relation to moving each child onto the next level (knowing where they were, where they are and where they need to go next). The commitment to educating the whole child also requires a rigorous and evidence-based play pedagogy.

Child development and neuroscience confirm comprehensibly that play pedagogy is essential for educating the child (and the whole child) in the early childhood years (see also Chapter 3). Expertise about the developing child and associated play theories provides the basis for an informed body of knowledge upon which educators are able to make empowered decisions about children's lives. The challenge early childhood educators face, as a profession, is the dilution of the importance of child development and a lack of education in the theories of play and play pedagogy. This can translate into non-rigorous teaching and learning through play, resulting in play that has an emphasis upon children's interests or themes dressed up to look like so-called 'projects'. The emphasis has shifted dangerously away from what used to be early childhood's defining motto, 'The process rather than the end product'. Now we see the movement towards the end product having to be installed, mounted on a wall, displayed in portfolios, described, narrated and shown off without attention to detail or the description of actual learning.

What this has inadvertently resulted in is a new generation of educators who, through no fault of their own, describe what a child has made or represented but have little idea of the child's skill, development, maturation, aspects of self-regulation or anything else that may require some depth of analysis. Descriptions being copied and pasted from outcomes such as 'Developing a sense of community and well-being while playing with "friend" in the sandpit on a project about volcanoes', hardly reflects a degree-holding educator's supposed body of knowledge of literacy, numeracy, thinking skills, oral language, body coordination, speech, hearing, handedness or other important considerations in a child's development. Writing reports, for example, that a child is being extended through their interest without any mention of an underlying intention for learning or skill acquisition has the potential to lower the overall standard of early childhood education.

Play in itself could cover a whole book. It is an entire discipline and this chapter is not designed to provide the overarching details of the discipline of play but rather to give a brief review of the theories of play and play pedagogy and key elements of play as a pedagogy. Alongside this we show how Walker Learning draws upon theories of play as the basis for its teaching and learning approach. This chapter is also intended to remind us of where we should be extending our reading and developing our skills and understandings further.

In terms of Walker Learning this chapter cannot be viewed in isolation but needs to be critically considered in combination with the other chapters in this book. In particular, the chapters that build on this chapter are intentional teaching (Chapter 2), setting up and creating an intentional and engaging learning environment (Chapter 6) and planning and documentation (Chapter 7). It is the combination of these deep understandings and systems that underpin Walker Learning as a rigorous evidence-based play pedagogy for early childhood education. We invite you to read on!

Play-based pedagogy

Play-based curriculum is meant to be intentional for learning, not about starting and ending and extending children's interests. Walker Learning is very clear that intention for learning comes first, the body of knowledge about the developing child comes first, process through open-ended material and provocations comes first, and that projects are not only unnecessary but incongruent with the developing child's need for hypothesis testing, exploring and developing skills and understanding in a context relative to how they view the world. In any case, why have children 'doing' projects in early childhood when this is what they will be doing for the next seven years of primary school?

Walker Learning uses children's lives and culture to build around and upon the intentions that are already firstly defined by child development and cultural appropriateness. Evidence drawn from neuroscience and developmental psychology are key platforms that place play curriculum as the foundation.

Walker Learning does not start from a mind map with a child's interest in the middle or a project about the Silvan Dam or a mini beast or sustainability. It starts from setting up a range of learning play areas based around what is developmentally appropriate through play, open-ended experiences that reflect the cultures and diversity of the community from which the children come. From that starting point, it becomes obvious what the children are interested in, as they construct, chat and play.

Implementation of Walker Learning requires an understanding and knowledge of play as a learning tool. This is an educational tool that has been examined and researched for many decades. Despite a general view of children and their play as frivolous, fun or undirected, many researchers over the years have presented successful theories and perspectives on play, and there is a rich history of using play as a learning tool. While each theorist and perspective reflects a range of different interpretations and emphases on children's learning and play, there are fundamental understandings about the nature of play and children's learning that are important for educators when exploring teaching and learning strategies within a play-based approach. These understandings are examined in the following sections of this chapter.

There are many different forms of play and investigations. Walker Learning provides a broad range of experiences and types of play so that children are immersed in a rich range of thinking, oral language, and literacy and numeracy experiences alongside opportunities to consolidate their social and emotional maturity. It is pertinent here to remind the reader of the broad-based perspective of what it means to be literate and numerate in early childhood education, such as communicating, self-expression (through multiple mediums), dramatising, storytelling, singing, role play and mathematical concepts. Literacy and numeracy are not formal but they are explicit and embedded within early childhood play-based curriculum.

Types of play

Imaginative and socio-dramatic play

Children use a range of materials in fantasy, in creating and representing their own ideas and understandings through imaginative play. In acting out, imagining and representing through play, their thinking and oral language skills are enhanced. This is one of the major ways in which children construct, make sense of and understand their world.

Constructive and investigative play

Children require hands-on, concrete materials, such as Lego®, Mobilo®, blocks, collage and interest tables with which they can construct, design and create a range of representations from their own imaginations.

Explorative play

This is the type of play where children are investigating the properties of things; finding out, exploring the environment, trying things out, often with mediums such as water, magnets, sand and magnifying glasses.

Sensory play

This is a very important part of children's learning. Children require sensory experiences through things such as water, clay, finger paint, aroma and touch. This is often an area that is neglected in the learning environment and is particularly useful with children's emotions, helping them to be calm and to have a safe outlet.

Stages of play

For many decades of research and through recent studies in neuroscience, we are reminded again that the thinking and perception of children's minds and processing is not the same as in adults. Cognition, processing, assimilating and making sense of materials, resources and concepts requires the developing brain to approach play from a number of different perspectives based upon experience and cognition. Stages of play are a general guide for the development of these cognitive processes that are influenced by age and prior opportunities and experiences.

Onlooker play

We are often concerned if we observe a child who is watching others and not joining in with their work or interactions. This can be a legitimate stage of a child's development. They are watching, taking information in, but not quite ready to engage or enter the play themselves. Even as adults, we at times take a step back to observe others.

Solitary play

This is the stage where children will work alone and attempt to keep themselves slightly removed from others. They engage in their own world of play and investigation and are neither aware nor interested in others at this time.

Parallel play

Children work alongside others, are aware of the play and interactions of others but predominantly are still working at their investigation. They may at times speak or interact minimally with others, but this is most often if they are interrupted by someone else or require one of the resources being used by another child. This stage is quite frequent and evident in children as they move from preschool to school.

Associative play

This stage reflects maturing cognitive development. Children are slightly less egocentric and are much more aware of others. They may work together on similar investigations at times and can take particular roles in their play and work. However, it is not as mature or refined as the next stage (cooperative). This stage is often confused with cooperative interaction and work.

Cooperative play

This is a very mature aspect of cognition. It occurs mostly in children moving into Year 2 or 3. It requires some degree of empathic understanding and a wider range of perceptions of others' feelings and needs. It is not a type of interaction that we would aim for in preschool or the early years of school, although opportunities through play will reflect some children moving into this stage during Year 2.

Walker Learning and stage of play

In the early years, children will often work individually in solitary play, and at other times in parallel and associative play. A key feature of Walker Learning is that it encourages and allows children to work on their own and in association with others. It does not expect or force children to work cooperatively together.

One of the educator's roles is to provide a rich range of opportunities for children to explore, investigate, involve and engage in purposeful, personalised and meaningful experiences, so that a number of different types of play, thinking, reasoning and understanding can occur.

Play used as a teaching and learning tool is not 'free play'. We do not just allow children to play when the real work is finished, or employ play to help children settle in. Play is always purposeful, linked to learning intentions and is the major strategy for teaching and learning. Play must be viewed as the main vehicle for learning to occur and as the child's work, not to be viewed by the child as a novelty.

Some key characteristics of play

Child-initiated play

Child-initiated play does not mean the adult cannot suggest, prompt, guide or scaffold in particular directions. However, at some stage, in some way, the child must be able to engage in a purposeful investigation that is of authentic interest to them. As Kelly-Byrne writes, 'The dramatic play of children is an alluring and incredibly complex kind of behaviour that is likely to encompass most, if not all, of a child's resources and integrate them into a whole' (1989, p. 212).

Symbolic play

This usually involves some element of pretend, imagination or role play. Through the exploration of a range of materials or equipment provided for the children, each child may create or reflect a particular role, medium or investigation that is representative to them of something in real life. For instance, a child may use a wooden block as a mobile phone, or a piece of long grass as a pirate's sword, or a cotton ball as a little puppy.

Play as a process not just an end product

The investigation, creation or work of a child may not necessarily always have to result in an end product. The process itself may be providing the practice of skills, thinking, creating, imagining or simply engaging in an experience that is purposeful and meaningful to the child at the time. The emphasis of a child's exploration in an experience in Walker Learning is related to skill acquisition and process – not a completed item or an end product.

Play is owned by the child not the adult

The play or experience belongs to the child. The adult may scaffold, intervene, extend, make suggestions or provide a direction. However, the child views the play or investigation as his or hers.

Play is active and creative and avoids worksheets and cloned expectation

Play involves the child being actively engaged in an exploration that is purposeful and investigative. It will involve some element of creativity and provides the opportunity for children to demonstrate their own ideas, understandings or needs. Play should not reflect an approach where each child has to make the same cloned egg or daffodil or clock. It is the child's mind, the child's skill and the child's learning, not the educator's.

Play involves children creating experiences that reflect their own interests. Colouring in pre-drawn stencilled shapes, cut-outs and cloned artwork is not part of Walker Learning or other evidence-based play-based curriculum.

Play reflects the interests of children for educators to scaffold learning

A major aspect of play-based curriculum is that play experiences are the basis for teaching and learning. Adults watch, observe, listen and talk with the children in order to ascertain what interests, ideas and directions the children can be encouraged to pursue as part of the learning process. It is sometimes known as the emergent curriculum – watching to see what ideas the children reflect or respond to, and then scaffolding the learning and skills from those interests (Stacey 2009). However, skills, learning and intentions are the basis for learning, and setting up play experiences and children's interests are merely used as springboards to help children acquire skills. Educators should not think the aim is to use a child's interest for the sake of the interest. That is not what Walker Learning is about.

Play is purposeful

The play and learning of the child involves them in a purposeful, constructive exploration or investigation that may be planned for, reflected on and linked for the child to their learning and interests.

Play involves literacy and numeracy

Literacy and numeracy are embedded within most life experiences. Walker Learning recognises the richness and breadth of literacy and numeracy through the range of children's play and investigations.

Educators utilise these experiences to link explicitly back to literacy and numeracy understandings and skills.

Play promotes social skills

Through engaging in investigative play-based learning experiences, children will sometimes work independently and at times in association with others. Through role play, acting out, problem solving, dealing with conflicts, trying out different tasks, negotiating, turn-taking, speaking and listening to each other, Walker Learning provides a rich range of social opportunities that are authentic and embedded within the natural way of interacting. There is no need to provide specific and separate social skills instruction, as this occurs naturally through play.

Play promotes oral language

Oral language is a critical element of the early years of learning. The most effective means to promote oral language is to provide a rich range of opportunities for children to engage with each other, to experiment and practise with words, language and conversation.

In dramatic play, social interactions, solving problems together and reflecting together at the end of each session on their play and learning, oral language is significantly enhanced. Oral language is also developed when children have the opportunity to engage in repeat conversations about the same things with adults (Copple & Bredekamp 2009). The development of oral language underpins all aspects of learning and is the major contributor to a child's comprehension.

Children's thinking processes through play

A number of key aspects of thinking and lifelong learning skills are facilitated through children actively engaged in learning through play. Some of these skills include:

- a range of thinking skills:
  - reasoning
  - perspective taking
  - problem solving
  - lateral thinking
  - divergent thinking
- oral language
- mathematical understandings and experiences
- literacy
- self-regulation and self-expression
- intrinsic motivation
- skill acquisition and practice
- self-initiation and decision making
- responsibility
- questioning
- reflecting
- resilience.

Links between learning, teaching and play

Play provides the most natural and meaningful means by which children can construct knowledge and understandings, practise skills, immerse themselves naturally in a broad range of literacy and numeracy, and engage in productive and intrinsically motivated learning environments. The children's interests provide great 'leaping-off' points for educators who can use these interests to introduce skills and understandings.

International research confirms that teaching and learning tools must be relevant and appropriate to the child's stage of maturity in order to sustain learning in meaningful ways, to promote an intrinsic approach to children's learning as well as to help children see that learning is not separate from life, but is an integral part of life (Lindsey 1998). Many studies highlight that creative, open and active learning environments produce happier children, less behavioural disruption and significantly engaged children who learn productively, sustain their learning over the long term and can transfer the skills they acquire to a range of different learning situations (Copple & Bradekamp 2009; Marcon 2003).

Summary

The key aims of this chapter are to show that:

- within play, there are many subsets or different types of play and learning that are occurring
- play is the most effective means for providing rich, diverse thinking and oral language, social skills and problem solving
- children's play reflects different levels of maturity
- play as a pedagogy must be planned for, directed by and facilitated by the educator
- play has been researched for many decades in relation to the significance it holds in children's lives, including for social, emotional, psychological and intellectual development and learning
- play is a natural way of children exploring their environment and learning about themselves and their world
- many skills are acquired through children's active exploration and investigation of their world
- play-based curriculum requires intention
- play-based curriculum is based upon a body of knowledge and expertise on how children learn and acquire skills through play
- play-based curriculum requires scaffolding through adults and learning environments
- play-based curriculum in Walker Learning is about the process of skill and learning, not about themes or projects of content
- play-based curriculum is open-ended and does not include stencilled artwork, cloned artwork or predesigned art to copy
- play-based curriculum in Walker Learning does not place emphasis upon displaying children's art or work, but emphasises the processes involved and the attempts, experiences and active investigations of learning and exploration
- play-based curriculum encourages attention to detail in all provocations, material and resources, both indoors and outdoors.

Suggested resources

Elkind, D 2007, *The power of play: learning what comes naturally*, DeCapo Press, Philadelphia.

Golinkoff, RM, Hirsh-Pasek, K & Eyer, D 2004, *Einstein never used flashcards: how our children really learn – and why they need to play more and memorize less*, Rodale Books, New York.

Wood, E & Attfield, J 2005, *Play, learning and the early childhood curriculum*, 2nd edn, Paul Chapman Publishing, London.

Chapter 6

Creating an intentional and engaging learning environment

'Education is a natural process carried out by the child and is not acquired by listening to words but by experience in the environment.'

Maria Montessori

Introduction

The learning environment is described in some education theories as the 'third teacher' (for examples of this concept in action, see http://www.thethirdteacher.com) and is a critical component of a high-quality early childhood education. The aim of an intentional and engaging learning environment is to promote a sense of wonder, exploration, investigation and interest in a rich range of materials, resources and opportunities in which the child can engage. The learning environment also motivates and creates opportunities for children to learn and develop skills. It aims to assist with the acquisition of skills and learning for children.

> *To ensure that learning, skills and development are progressing, how we establish and maintain the learning environment is one of the most important elements of an early childhood educator's role.*

Attention to detail, daily provocations, being clear what skills and learning will be facilitated, and knowing how we can add to the learning play area to provoke further investigation, all ensure that children are not just 'playing with their own interests' but learning and extending and developing. This is what separates the early childhood educator from the babysitter.

In early childhood settings particularly (and increasingly in many primary settings), the outdoor environment is viewed as having equal value and importance as part of learning, skill acquisition and development. Traditionally, in primary schools the outdoor 'play' at lunchtime and morning playtime was viewed as a time for eating, free play and for teachers to take a break if they were not on playground duty. Traditionally, in early childhood settings, a great deal of appreciation and value has been placed upon the outdoor environment as a means for learning. However, a number of issues need to be further examined, including how well it is set up, how it is utilised and viewed by educators, and how rich and broad the range of provocations are that are placed into the outdoor areas.

Without the right type of learning environment, and a range of play learning areas, set out in ways that are conducive to the development and age of the children, with the right types of provocations, materials and resources, the educator may come dangerously close to simply providing a play experience that can be found in any home or backyard, and which lacks the intention, expertise, scaffolding and extension of learning that is required.

Key learning experiences

The learning environment is constructed with a number of key learning experiences, and in Walker Learning these are referred to as key learning areas; these are fluid and can change a little depending upon the ages in a room, but are a guide to demonstrate that, as we discussed in intentional teaching in Chapter 2, our starting point is not setting up each area based on children's interests, but carefully considering what types of areas promote what types of skills, opportunities to experience new concepts and to enhance elements of learning including open-ended, non-explicit aspects of literacy, numeracy, science, nature, socialisation, emotional regulation, language skills, perspective taking, motor coordination, spatial awareness and self-concept, among many other factors. The learning play areas are not so simplistic as to just extend a child's interest in dinosaurs, for example. This is a critical point that needs to be clearly addressed and understood when setting up the learning environment.

The learning play areas are established and remain in general areas of consistency throughout the term. However, on a daily/weekly/monthly/term basis, slight modifications will be made by both children and educators based upon a skill to be extended, an additional provocation being added in, or an interest of a child that can be placed into or alongside one or more of the areas to add value and to assist with engagement. But the interest itself is not what the experience per se is actually all about.

The learning play areas are based on fundamental theories of child development and neuroscience. Each area takes on the specific local cultural and community relevance of where the early childhood centre is situated. However, the rigour of the learning environment should be such that each learning area has, in the first instance, specific intentions, purpose for skill and development, and is open-ended. From this starting position the learning area will evolve over time as a result of constant reflection by the educator on how the children engage in the area and the learning intentions.

The key learning play areas include as a minimum: dramatic play, tinkering, sensory, construction, reading, collage, literacy resource, numeracy resource, painting/drawing and mark making, carpentry, climbing and swinging, science and nature (see Figure 6.1). The learning environment (indoors and outdoors) will have at least one of each learning area, and in some cases there will be multiple experiences of the same learning area set up differently (such as multiple small sensory areas around the room and outside); this may be a little different in the babies and toddlers' learning play areas, which are discussed later in the chapter.

The learning play areas provide opportunities for children to explore and investigate a range of open-ended and engaging experiences. Educators add provocations into the learning play areas on a daily and weekly basis to promote development, skills and further learning (Figure 6.2). In Chapter 7 we discuss how the daily/weekly record and the statement of intent guide the educators when setting up the learning environment, provocations and scaffolding and modelling.

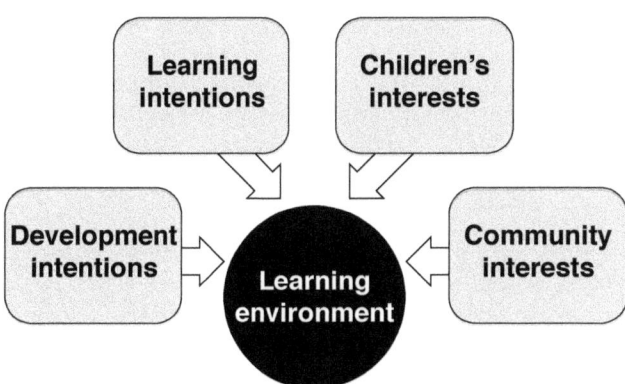

Figure 6.2 Educators add provocations from the four key planning elements into the learning play areas on a daily and weekly basis to promote development, skills and further learning.

Each key learning play area develops skills and opportunities in its own right even before additional provocations are planned or added (see Table 6.1); and each key learning play area is open-ended, thus helping each child to create and explore from their own construct and experience. There is no rotation method or need for each child to stay at one area or have practice or experience in every area.

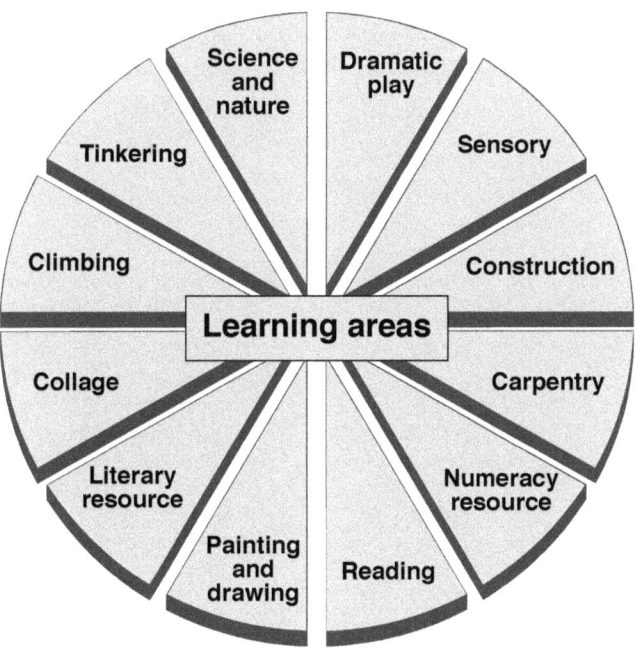

Figure 6.1 The learning environment is set up with the following key learning play areas: dramatic play, tinkering, sensory, construction, reading, collage, literacy resource, numeracy resource, painting/drawing and mark making, carpentry, climbing, science and nature.

Chapter 6 Creating an intentional and engaging learning environment 63

Table 6.1 Each key learning play area develops skills and opportunities in its own right even before additional provocations are planned or added

\multicolumn{5}{c}{Key elements and skill development of learning play areas}				
Dramatic play	**Sensory**	**Collage**	**Construction**	**Painting and drawing**
Dramatic play offers a whole range of skills and understandings about a wide range of roles and aspects of community life. Skill development includes: • oral language • dramatic self-expression (non-verbal) • therapeutic role play • thinking • social interaction • collaboration • perspective taking • literacy • numeracy • problem solving • reading • writing.	Sensory areas are extremely important for children. Sensory areas need to be presented in a range of different areas in multiple learning play areas for individual and small groups of children. Skill development includes: • fine motor development • eye–hand and muscle control • soothing and therapeutic value • oral language • artistic expression • nature • science • creativity.	Collage, constructing, making and pasting, is one of the most popular learning play areas. Skill development includes: • cognitive processing • problem solving • fine motor and muscle control • literacy and numeracy • perceptual development • imagination • resilience • persistence • planning, designing, thinking, measuring and adapting.	Construction involves blocks, Lego® (and other manipulative equipment), road signs, train tracks and as many construction and manipulative tools that are accessible and age appropriate. Skill development includes: • constructing • building • designing and mapping • perspective taking • measuring and balancing • oral language • collaborating • extending upon • mathematical and physics concepts • gross and fine motor development.	Painting and drawing provides a range of resources by which children explore mediums and forms of expression. All experiences are open-ended rather than stencils or cut-outs or colouring in. Skill development includes: • creativity • hand–eye coordination • fine motor skills • gross motor skills • planning • large- and small-scale creative self-expression • opportunities to cross the midline • left/right eye orientation • colour concepts.
Reading	**Science and nature**	**Tinkering and carpentry**	**Literacy resource**	**Numeracy resource**
Pre-reading opportunities with fact, fiction, rhyme and poetry. Time to read alone and alongside others in cosy tucked-away areas, outside and inside, in specifically designated reading areas. Skill development includes: • pre-reading cognition • storytelling • relaxing • relationship building • care of books • decision making.	Science and nature learning play areas provide opportunities for the exploration of science and the natural world. Skill development includes: • oral language • eye–hand coordination and muscle control • soothing and therapeutic value • experimentation • exploration of the properties of scientific investigation.	Carpentry is most usually an outdoor learning play area. However, tinkering is either indoors or outdoors. Safety goggles are a must. Objects can include old keys, radios, telephones, things to pull apart, the list in never-ending! Skill development includes: • conversation • experimentation • problem solving • fine motor skills • thinking • designing.	Literacy is part of everyday life – the literacy resource area contains tools of literacy: texts, clipboards, signs, children's writing, books, notes and opportunities to write, design and read.	Numeracy is also everywhere around us. The numeracy resource learning area is filled with tools of numeracy: stop watches, currency, dice, calculators, rulers, tape measures and abacus.

Traditionally in early childhood education, there have been minimal texts or books outside the reading area. It is important in many learning play areas that opportunities for writing, and books and clipboards are placed both indoors and outdoors so that literacy and numeracy are simply part of a child's early life, not something they have to wait formally for once they commence school.

The following sections provide a description of each key learning play area and the skills and opportunities these experiences offer in their own right.

Dramatic play

Children need many opportunities for dramatic play. This is a major way in which oral language and a range of other literacy and numeracy skills are developed, as well as problem solving, decision making, persistence, creative and lateral thinking, and perspective taking.

It should be noted that dramatic play occurs in many different areas of the learning environment, not just in a defined dramatic play area, but it is important and useful to have a defined dramatic play area that can facilitate a wide range of concepts and understandings. Dramatic play needs to occur both inside and outside. Inside it is often easier to set up an area, usually in a corner, and large enough for three to four children to work and create there. Dramatic play can also be encouraged through the use of dramatic props such as building blocks, Lego®, doll's houses, cosy corners to investigate, or 'pull-apart' tables with old computers.

Examples of dramatic play include:

- home corner
- supermarket
- post office
- airport
- hospital
- shop.

Children will also initiate ideas for dramatic play that may be based on a discussion with the educator. Educators may set up a dramatic play concept based on the interests and ideas of the children, or introduce a particular dramatic play focus depending on some of the issues or ideas the educator wishes to promote.

Dramatic play is one of the major strategies for promoting rich oral language both for children who have English as a first language and for children who have English as a second language. The language in dramatic play is rich, purposeful and authentic. Children are highly motivated and engaged and the vocabulary, grammar, articulation and listening skills are all highly evident in dramatic play.

Many numeracy and literacy skills are also enhanced and promoted through dramatic play. The provocations intentionally included in the learning areas will facilitate the development of these skills; for example, clocks, appointment pads, books and magazines.

Sensory

Sensory experiences are important for children. A sensory experience provides fine motor and hand–eye practice, and additionally allows children to experience creativity and be in tune with not just their thinking and academic skills but the sensory perception areas as well. The sensory perception areas of the brain require touch, sound and smell, and these areas are also very therapeutic for children, providing calmness for anxious children, and soothing, relaxing experiences for children who find it hard to self-soothe and self-calm.

At times sensory play can link directly to a literacy experience or it may simply be a means unto itself, which children may then extend. Sensory play may include:

- clay
- play dough
- water
- mud
- sand with a fragrance
- dirt with natural materials such as pine cones.

It is recommended that sensory experiences are provided in small trays or buckets to facilitate individual or small groups of children engaging in the experience. Sensory play is often included in other areas such as dramatic play and construction.

Sensory areas should be small and there should be many of them throughout the learning environment both inside and outside and not just contained to large water troughs or sand trays.

Collage

The collage area provides rich opportunities for a never-ending range of creativity, investigations and experimentation with materials, and is where much literacy and numeracy occurs. The area is usually two tables – but not joined together, perhaps L-shaped; this enables children to work in smaller groups. Collage provides a range of learning and skill opportunities for children and for educators to scaffold and model. Informal language can be used regarding size, shape and location such as beside, on top, how long and how much. Collage assists with children's basic fine motor, eye–hand and defining handedness control. It facilitates rich language and thinking and creative skills. It assists with fundamental life skills such as passing masking tape to a peer, taking turns with limited scissors and waiting one's turn.

Always provide access for children to a range of collage materials. These need to be stored and don't all have to be available each day, but children need to be aware there is a supply of different collage materials. Displaying and presenting the materials needs to create a sense of invitation, order, grouping and organisation, rather than just having everything stored in a large box or container that children cannot see. It also helps children to respect the materials and makes it easier for them to pack away.

The range of collage materials should also reflect variety and include, at different times, some of the following suggestions:

- natural materials such as gum nuts, pine cones, leaves, flowers, pebbles or feathers
- boxes of different sizes
- cardboard
- coloured paper
- cotton wool
- buttons
- ribbons.

The list is endless. Utilising parents to collect resources and joining something like a reverse art shop, as well as getting local shopkeepers to collect off-cuts, for instance, are invaluable ways of collecting materials.

Reading

Reading areas are used for relaxing, reading, researching, sharing information and storytelling. They should be quiet, attractive and defined spaces, which also reflect an exciting or inviting place for children to visit. Reading areas are best situated in quieter areas (both inside and outside) and should be presented as warm, cosy spaces and are often defined and contained by using netting, tents, cushions and sofas.

Sometimes children's own work may be included in the reading area. Children, as they grow older, may have drawn a story or told a story that can be included for them and others to look at.

Reading spaces should hold a range of non-fiction as well as fiction books that children can use. Children's own books, reflecting their interests, can be displayed as authentic and quality books for other children to share and read together. Other provocations may include pictures of family, culture, local landmarks and community events (with or without captions). These are fabulous for younger children too and for children who may be a little anxious.

Construction

This area promotes a range of skills including fine motor, language and conversation, design, thinking, collaboration, numeracy, investigation, problem solving, perspective, literacy, mapping, and the list goes on.

Children construct knowledge and understanding through hands-on creating. These experiences are an integral part of play pedagogies. Children need opportunities to develop, plan and represent ideas. These may at times relate to some particular part of an investigation, or may just be something that is useful and relevant to the child on that particular day.

Ensure there are resources such as Lego® or Mobilo® for children to work with. Provision of shelving or display spaces for works-in-progress encourage children to return to, extend and build on some of their investigations. It may be that photographs are taken of the works and used for pages in portfolios. Spaces for construction can be defined with masking tape on the floor in squares or circles or with mats as described below.

Blocks are one of the most versatile and constructive tools for children to use. Design work, planning, actual construction and the extension of dramatic play into the block area is rich and filled with many opportunities for the educator to scaffold numeracy and literacy.

Blocks are also very effective outside as part of dramatic play; they assist with motor coordination and children working alongside each other. High-quality blocks are imperative.

Spirit levels, tape measures, rulers, lots of additional materials and resources assist with building language and thinking, and enriching this area.

Science and nature

Science and nature investigations add value to learning through open-ended materials and resources. Exploration of the properties of scientific investigation as well as of the natural world contribute to curriculum areas and provide a rich and engaging way for children to learn.

The skills promoted in this area include: oral language, eye–hand coordination and muscle control; soothing and therapeutic value; experimentation and exploration of the properties of scientific investigation.

Using microscopes, magnifying glasses, scales, mirrors and lights, and adding different resources each week will continue to engage children deeply with their explorations and investigations.

Tinkering and carpentry

Carpentry is most usually an outdoor learning experience. However, tinkering is either indoors or outdoors. In the tinkering area the children can pull apart, undo, unlock and unwind – old keys and locks, radios, telephones, things to pull apart, the list is never-ending! Safety goggles in these areas are a must.

The outdoor carpentry area is an exciting and highly creative experience in which children can engage. For younger children this experience can be wood and glue, and for older children soft wood with hammer and nail (pliers to hold nails are good for children just beginning to hammer nails).

The skills promoted in tinkering and carpentry include: oral language (conversation), problem solving, fine motor skills, thinking, designing, perseverance and lateral thinking.

Literacy resource

Literacy is part of everyday life, and the learning environment should be filled with the tools of literacy: texts, clipboards, signs, children's writing, books, notes and opportunities to write, design and read. The environment should be filled with opportunities to use literacy in real, relevant and meaningful ways.

The literacy resource area is where the children come to use or collect the 'tools of literacy' – not for the child to come to 'do a literacy activity'. This area will include pens, papers, scissors and work-in-progress signs, pens, pencils, textas, envelopes/stamps, post box, clipboards, notepads, easel, a variety of plain and coloured paper, and photos.

Numeracy resource

Numeracy also is part of everyday life, and the learning environment should be filled with the tools of numeracy. The numeracy resource area is where the children come to use or collect the 'tools of numeracy' – not for the child to come to 'do a numeracy activity'. This area may include calculators, dice, egg timers, clocks, abacus, numbers, tape measures, rulers, cards, scales, money, clipboards and pencils.

Painting and drawing

Painting and drawing, and the use of clay, sand and soil are just a few of the means by which children explore mediums and forms of expression and exploration, and are fundamental in creative learning environments.

Painting easels are an effective tool for improving bilateral coordination, and both gross and fine motor skills. They are useful for promoting oral language, thinking, planning, and describing colour and shape concepts. A variety of mediums can be provided at the easels other than just paint. Pasting with a range of materials at the easels provides a different perspective in which children can explore and experiment. It is preferable to include two easels side by side so that they can be either a social and language experience for children or a solitary experience.

Outdoor learning

The outdoor learning area is considered to be as equal to indoor space, and is extremely important in learning for children. The use of outdoor space provides connectedness and continuity with the indoor experiences along with being an area in its own right. As with the indoor environment, the outdoor environment is developed with intention (related to development, learning and children's interests) and the use of provocations.

Establishing places to learn outside is a great way to ease the pressure children may feel being inside – many children, particularly boys, work more constructively and productively outside. Setting up an environment that allows children to move more freely and comfortably helps to ease some of the behaviour disruptions that can occur when children are working very closely together. It is desirable that children can move between inside and outside at times during the day and that the learning is viewed by them as being inside and outside.

Outdoor learning provides the opportunity for sensory experiences such as playing with water, sand and mud. Having 1 m × 1 m mats to work on outside helps children to be comfortable and to construct and build on a surface if they wish to. Mats also help to define spaces. All experiences that are provided inside can also be provided outside, including: collage, construction, books, wood and natural materials.

It is useful to have one table and a couple of chairs outside so that children can sit and chat with each other from time to time. They may do some group planning or design briefs before they commence their work.

Babies and toddlers

The babies and toddlers' learning play areas need to reflect a home-like environment with cosy chairs and sofas; as well as mats on the floor that are soft and that a baby would want to sit or roll or lie on. It should not look like a plastic assortment of a watered-down toddlers or kinder room. There should be lots of natural materials. It should feel like a living room at home with more things to do given they can't access other rooms in the house. The priorities for the babies and toddlers' learning play areas are relationships and attachment, consistent carers, primary attachment figures, cuddling, and flexible and individualised programs.

The babies' environment should reflect the following:

- couch for cuddling
- minimal tables
- opportunities to crawl:
  - on different surfaces
  - brushing past materials on the face
  - through and around
- lots of sensory experiences for the face – scarves, material
- lots of outdoors:
  - wind, sun, shadows
  - chimes
- aromatherapy, music
- slow pace
- regular exposure to everyday experiences (e.g. cooking)
- no group times, only one-on-one – reading, singing, rhythm.

The toddlers' environment should reflect:

- opportunities to develop independence – but still lots of nurturing and cuddling

- primarily solitary play phase – lots of the same material, not expecting to share
- should not look like a mini preschool room
- nooks, crannies, cosy, indoor, outdoor
- minimal tables – predominance of floor experiences
- low tables
- couch for cuddling
- indoor–outdoor
- practice at climbing, sliding, swinging
- slow pace
- regular exposure to everyday experiences
- construction – pull apart and put together
- lots of sensory experiences
- reading area – for reading, singing, rhyming
- dramatic play – home corner and dress-ups
- collage – small area.

Key features of an engaging and intentional learning environment

Children require an environment that:

- reflects and respects their ideas, interests, strengths and needs
- provides creative and open-ended learning experiences as opposed to cloned art work
- provides opportunities to work or play alone and alongside others
- promotes a sense of authentic choice and belonging
- links learning outside and inside
- provides a sense of calm and 'containment'.

Within the learning environment, children need opportunities to:

- self-regulate and self-select
- act independently at times
- learn pack-up and set-up responsibilities
- choose from a rich range of materials
- work alongside others if so desired.

The way the materials are presented, stored and displayed, and how the environment is set up, helps to attract and engage children to achieve these opportunities and to work competently and responsibly within the environment. The key features of an early childhood play-based learning environment are:

- open-ended learning experiences
- creativity and imagination
- intentional/purposeful ideas encouraged
- choice and range of areas for children to move between
- the adult role in scaffolding is important
- it is reflective of children, culture and new experiences
- provocations are added to extend skills and learning
- it reflects developmentally and culturally appropriate materials and provocations that assist with creativity, learning, concepts and skill acquisition
- learning areas set children up to succeed not to fail
- learning areas should be available to children for most of the day.

The following section outlines the principles guiding the set-up of the learning environment along with some practical tips and strategies.

Defining the learning experiences and spaces

In their early years, children still like time to work and play on their own. This actually helps with concentration and attending to tasks, and limits interruptions from others. Learning areas should reflect the philosophy that all children, spending up to six or more hours together in the same space, require the respect of sometimes having more of their own personal space.

Defining the learning areas helps children to stay calm and focused – defining and containing the space is known as providing 'psychological containment'. It also helps children to choose materials independently. Defining the space is achieved through the use of the physical environment resources to make cosy corners, nooks and crannies (think of little rooms within the room). Big open spaces, tall ceilings and undefined open areas create a setting where children will start running around, not being focused and not feeling secure. This is why defining the space is such a critical component of the learning environment. In addition, the space can be 'contained' by the use of resources such as curtains, cane, trellis, cupboards, table coverings and mats.

Individual mats (approximately 1 m x 1 m) also help to define spaces for individual children. At times children may wish to join mats together to form larger groups. They can also be used outside so children have something comfortable to sit on as they work. In an average group size (23 children), each room could have 5–10 mats. They are easily stacked and stored. Mats encourage children to work either in solitary, parallel or associative play. These opportunities and different types of work and learning are important for all children.

Attention to detail

Prioritising attention to detail when setting up a learning play area is a critical element of achieving a high-quality and rigorous learning area. Greater attention to detail is generally required in play-based curriculum. It is this element that makes the difference in order to responsively scaffold, be intentional, seize a moment, introduce a new vocabulary for a child, introduce a new mathematical concept, model some writing, or extend a new concept. The colour section in this book provides examples of attention to detail in learning play areas facilitating deep thinking, broad vocabulary and rich engagement where learning can occur.

Attention to detail is not only an important part of the initial setting up of the learning play areas indoors and outdoors, but is also important in the daily adding of provocations, which is an imperative part of the play-based curriculum. In Walker Learning particularly, it is the attention to detail in the initial set up and daily provocations that enriches and deepens the play into intentional learning.

For instance, if the dramatic play is going to be a home corner, then real crockery and cutlery, real placements, real saucepans, note paper, phones, newspapers, pens, clipboards, magazines, recipe books, scales, implements for cooking, words on labels, posters, aprons, bags, and so on, should all be set up and displayed in a tidy, organised and aesthetically pleasing way. If it is a collage area, it needs to be set up creatively, with everything labelled, sorted, neat and tidy, with something to provoke interest for children to make them want to see what might be new in the area.

Attention to detail is also related to how the educator uses layers, levels, colours, textures, light and depth in setting up the learning area – see the following section.

Layers, levels, colours, textures, light and depth

The following points provide ideas about how to embrace attention to detail when setting up a learning play area. The design elements listed are important in their own right, but are also all interconnected and cannot be seen in isolation from one another:

- The learning areas need to be *well defined* in a 3D way to create a 'room within a room' look and feel. Furniture placement, shelving, room dividers, fabric, plants and mirrors can achieve this. These spaces need to have depth rather than a '2D sit-at space' perspective. Educators should aim for snug 'child sized' spaces.

- Depth is achieved through *low* overhead canopies, material/fabric – folded, layered and hung in, around and on things. Cushions, mirrors, lighting (lamps – both small and floor lamps), light boxes, mats and rugs all add depth to the area.

- Layers and levels add to both of the above points, and create interest, and different engagement and focal points. Many vertical levels should be considered, such as the floor space, rugs, small platforms, varying sized blocks, stools, shelves and tables.

- The backdrop of each space can really make or break the scene – backdrop is an important detail. For instance, if children can look through to another area this often detracts and distracts children from the one play space to the next.

- Complementary or contrasting colours and textures should be explored and experimented with to get the right look and feel. The inclusion of lamps and soft lights help calm an area while also providing containment of a space.

- Grouping things in odd numbers and in a non-symmetrical way is also recommended. The rule of three (sometimes known as the rule of odds) is a principle used in various aspects of design: architecture, graphic design, photography. The basic idea of the rule is that details and objects that are arranged or grouped in odd numbers are more appealing, memorable and effective than even-numbered pairings. While it is easier to create symmetry by balancing elements in twos, odd numbers create harmony and force movement and visual interest.

Invitation to engage

The invitation to engage is the final touch that an educator makes to a learning environment before the children begin. The invitation to engage is a series of small adjustments made to a learning area that makes the area look like 'someone has been in there and has just started playing' – it is the invitation to 'come on in and play'. Invitation to engage shifts the view of the learning play area from being stark, sterile and static to … exciting, tempting, enticing and dynamic. The invitation to engage may be the way the paper is set out in the collage area at different angles or sequences, a tape measure is draped or curled and is in a prominent position of an area, some shading on a paper with a crayon, clipboards set up with the pencil at an angle, a few blocks set up as a beginning of a construction – all these things are tempting the child to pick up, explore, begin, think and engage.

Resources and materials

Resources provided in the learning environment need to be neat, tidy and categorised. Keeping things categorised, organised and tidy also models respect for the children. Real items are always used in preference to plastic options. The materials and resources are there to create visual prompts for thinking – the experiences need to be visually inviting. It is almost as if the learning experience beckons the child to come in, touch, explore, think, enjoy and wonder! Importantly, all learning experiences need to be print rich (with books, words, clipboards, pencils).

Learning experiences should be set up ideally on the floor or low tables without regular height tables.

Group time area

Children need time to meet together, to share ideas, to reflect, to engage in explicit instruction sessions and to spend time chatting with the educator. Each room requires some space where the children can come together. It does not always have to be at the front of the room, and educators are encouraged to set up the room first and then find a space for group time.

In early childhood education, group times ideally are short and invitational so that all children are not forced to come to group time. This can often cause stress for children and they may already be happily and richly engaged in their learning elsewhere.

Group times may be to start the day, which we call 'tuning in', or to end the day, which we call 'reflection'; they may sometimes be done in small groups, not whole groups, and sometimes not done at all.

Many educators believe that a whole group time is always necessary or somehow a major means of preparation for school. Having an area where children know that they meet, talk, have stories or songs is part of the ritual and pattern of life, but it does not need always to be compulsory.

Certainly in the babies and toddlers' learning play areas, it is inappropriate for formal group times where children are often crying and crawling away from the group or stressed because they are being made to sit still on the mat.

For three to five year olds, there can be great joy in coming together at times to share in a story or song or game. But we need to remember that all children are different and we should not be forcing all children at this young age to come to group time or causing them stress.

Resources for linking play to literacy and numeracy

The list below gives a brief overview of some of the materials and resources that can help to extend and scaffold the learning experiences within literacy and numeracy. Provide in a number of areas (including block play and dramatic play):

- writing paper
- clipboards
- lists
- notepads
- journals
- portfolios
- easels with paper and pens
- literacy resource area with pens, pencils, paper, stamps, letters and envelopes.

Open-ended experiences rather than closed activities

As discussed in Chapters 2 and 3 it is the process that needs to be the fundamental element of play-based curriculum, rather than end products or content-heavy projects that are often driven by adults. Part of honouring the process rather than the end product is to provide open-ended as opposed to closed experiences.

Open-ended experiences are where:

- children can take materials, resources and props and create, imagine and take their play and investigation wherever they want to while learning at the same time
- there is no predetermined outcome or preconceived idea of what has to be made or how it has to look
- the educator already knows that the materials and experiences will promote skills. It doesn't matter what the end product is, because the skills and processes are what is most important.

An open-ended learning play area, display, resource or expectation provides a range of materials, resources, equipment and tools that the children are able to utilise in ways in which they can use their own:

- imaginations
- skills
- ideas
- creativity
- prior experience
- thoughts.

A closed activity is characterised by the following:

- there is a prototype provided
- a stencil or pre-drawn or re-cut-out shape for children already provided
- an instruction:
  - on how to cut or draw or colour it in
  - that says, for example, 'Today we are all going to make a Christmas tree and here is the shape'
  - that says, for example, 'Today we are all making an Easter Bunny and it has to have these ears and eyes and tail we have made for you'.

Closed activities:

- predetermine how and what the child must make or create
- stifle and inhibit thinking, imagination and motivation
- perpetuate a belief in learning that everyone is the same, thinks the same and has to be the same
- do not reflect diversity or personalised learning.

Using a rich range of writing and drawing materials, pasting and construction are the key ingredients that promote children's oral language, literacy, numeracy, creativity and initiative. The use of cloned artwork, stencilled ideas, pre-drawn ideas and colouring-in sheets is unnecessary.

Ensure that materials can be mixed together. For example, placing Lego®, animals or writing materials alongside blocks helps promote a richer investigation.

Promoting persistence

An important part of the work of children is to return to it, to persist, to work further on some of their tasks and to feel a sense of pride in their attempts. The provision of some special display space or shelving for storing works in progress is important to children. They are encouraged to respect each other's work as well as to continue their own work, and not just work at something or complete something in 10 minutes.

Some key points for consideration:

- Not all children must have a table to sit at or a chair to sit on.

- Play and work stations should remain where they are, and not require packing away each day.

- Provision of some space for displays of investigations and self-selection for children should be attempted.

- The nature of the experiences should not require an adult to be present in order for the experiences to be productive or for the children to be able to work on them. For example, avoid sewing or threading experiences unless you have an additional adult to assist.

Information technology in early childhood education

As reported in Chapter 3, the early childhood years is a time when children need 'concrete hands-on experiences'. Consistent with this evidence the use of computers and iPads should be either minimal or not at all. Children already have extensive time on electronic devices often at the expense of other important opportunities to play. Moreover, the children who most need oral language experience and practice and hands-on social interaction are often the ones who gravitate to the computers most. In the early childhood centre, electronic devices should not be used for games and cannot be justified as being an 'educational experience'.

Summary

The key aims of this chapter are to show that:

- the learning space is both indoors and outdoors
- the learning environment must reflect individual spaces as well as contained and defined spaces that do not need to be dominated by tables
- a full range of different experiences should always be provided for, including dramatic play, sensory play, writing, reading and construction
- educators should avoid having too many pieces of work hanging from the ceiling and over-stimulating children with excessive visual stimuli
- the provision of open-ended materials promotes creativity
- cloned artwork, colouring-in and cloned worksheets are not used
- literacy and numeracy become part of the natural way of life through having clipboards, a literacy and numeracy resource area, and books and things to write on both inside and outside everywhere
- children should always have access to a full range of materials so the educator does not have to be interrupted repeatedly during each session
- attention to detail is an integral and imperative aspect of Walker Learning with rich provocations in each area which are altered slightly each day
- daily provocations should be provided for children and sometimes by children
- children's lives and interests and culture are part of the learning play areas but not the key starting point
- children should be free to choose where they work/explore
- children should not be forced to sleep or lie down.

Suggested resources

Bass, S & Walker, K (DVD), *Setting up and engaging and intentional learning environment.*

The Third Teacher, http://www.thethirdteacher.com.

Dramatic play areas

Dramatic play experiences provide real-life experiences that are culturally appropriate. Real items related to these experiences are essential for rich and deep engagement. Plastic and/or fake items are not used. These areas must have literacy (such as books, maps, menus) and numeracy (such as clocks, phones, money) provocations.

Sensory areas

Multiple sensory areas around the learning play area are essential – these are mostly small experiences available for only one or two children. Other sensory experiences can be incorporated into other learning play areas. Provocations typically include magnifying glass, clipboard and pencil, a variety of resources, textures and layers, mirrors, spices, herbs, soft lights, and print-rich and numeracy provocations.

Collage areas

The collage area presents a variety of easily accessible, visible, categorised and ordered resources. The inclusion of natural materials adds sensory elements (smell, texture, colour) and a more natural feel to the area.

This area does not include any stencils, cloned art work, instructions or directions on how to make things.

Reading areas

Reading areas are quiet, cosy, tranquil spaces where children can relax and engage. A variety of resources and provocations such as books, clipboards, children's work, cushions, artefacts, soft lights, soft mats and overhead canopies typically define this area.

Construction area

Construction areas are the places for construction of all sorts and have a base of various building resources. Provocations typically include spirit levels, tape measures, clipboards, print-rich resources (books, signs), small notepads and pencils, construction signs, and workers hats and vests. Additional props include draped material, plants and stones.

Attention to detail

Placement of tape measure, clipboard with pencil 'ready', arrangement of construction items and spirit levels should be to the front of the area and create a sense of someone having just started.

Science and nature areas

Science and nature areas are non-themed resources and provocations that include opportunities to investigate, explore the properties of objects, wonder and manipulate, to enhance vocabulary and thinking, and to experience the scientific and natural world. As with all areas, literacy and numeracy provocations are essential.

Attention to detail

These areas provide a variety of textures, and mats and materials add to the layers. The backdrops (fish tank and trellis with material) help contain and define the space. Materials and resources are set out intentionally to provoke engagement and thinking.

Tinkering areas

The tinkering area contains any items that can be pulled apart, undone, deconstructed and reconstructed, and needs to contain all the tools of the trade! Typical provocations include workers hats, vests, safety goggles, earmuffs, spanners, screwdrivers, pliers, hammers, nuts, bolts, locks and keys. Numeracy and literacy provocations typically include spirit levels, books, booklets, clipboards, signs, labels, tape measures and rulers.

Literacy resource areas

The literacy resource area is where children can find all the tools of literacy to use in their investigations. It is not a place where children go to 'do' literacy activities or to practise their literacy skills. Literacy resource areas classically include letters, words, envelopes, paper (varied in size, weight and colour), notebooks, pads, cards, clipboards, literacy resource books, pencils, textas and post boxes.

Numeracy resource areas

The numeracy resource area is where children can find all the tools of numeracy to use in their investigations. It is not a place where children go to 'do' numeracy activities. Numeracy resource areas classically include tape measures, rulers, egg timers, stopwatches, clocks, cards, calculators, abacus, protractors, clipboards, numerals, maths resource books, scales and items such as buttons and dice.

Painting and drawing areas

Painting and drawing areas always have a range of implements for mark making. It is essential that pencils are always sharpened, paints and pots are always cleaned and a range of experiences are provided. Attention is needed to ensure that the resources used are appropriate (e.g. ensuring the crayons, paint and pencils are complementary for use on paper, bark and materials).

Attention to detail

Paper has been set out ready and is framed with coloured paper or a mat. Implements should be ready at hand to entice the child to engage. Plants add depth and colour and soften the area.

Outdoor learning play areas

The outdoor learning play area is considered to be equal to indoor space, and is extremely important in learning for children. The use of outdoor space provides connectedness and continuity with the indoor experiences along with being an area in its own right. All the areas of the indoor environment can be part of the outdoor environment. As with the indoor environment, the outdoor environment is developed with intention (related to development, learning and children's interests), use of provocations, attention to detail and the invitation to engage.

Babies and toddlers' learning play areas

Dramatic play and sensory experience

Natural materials (autumn leaves and logs), soft lights, material, wooden figurines and mirrors provide a contained space, a range of textures, and visual and physical depth and calm.

Sensory and gross motor skills

Babies and toddlers need a range of opportunities to crawl on different surfaces, to brush past material with their face, and to crawl through and around objects. Babies and toddlers love the sensory experience on their face such as scarves, material and leaves.

Reading area

Reading areas need to be cosy and quiet, and offer a range of reading resources that are appropriate for babies and toddlers. The material canopy enhances the cosy, contained feel of the area. The rugs and cushions also define space and make the area cosy. Shelving for books adds depth while also displaying books that are easily accessible. Plants add a sensory component and soften the area.

Sensory area

Sensory experiences are essential for babies and toddlers. Small experiences are set up for only one or two children. The sensory medium (sand, water, clay, etc) in each area is developed with provocations and props such as wooden animals, plants, lamps (which provide calming and different light perspectives), photos, books, magnifying glasses, arches and natural materials.

Science-nature area

The science-nature area provides an eclectic mix of science-nature provocations, print-rich resources (books, clipboards), tape measures, natural materials, layers, textures and depth by using synthetic grass, a wooden case and backdrop.

Couch/chair for cuddling and one-on-one time

A couch or chair is where the educator can spend one-on-one time with a baby or toddler. Reading, singing, talking and sharing emotions (delight, wonder, joy) are all important in strengthening the attachment of the child to the educator.

Chapter 7

Planning, documentation and assessment: want your life back?

'Children must be taught how to think, not what to think.'

Margaret Mead

Introduction

The early childhood profession in Australia has gone through great change in structure, management and accountability over the past decade. The introduction of the National Quality Framework (NQF) and the transfer of early childhood education into the Education portfolio have been significant influences in this process. This has provided the platform for early childhood education to be acknowledged and endorsed in its own right as being the most important education years of an individual's life (Akbari & McCuaig 2014; Sylva et al. 2004). While these provide positive opportunities and change for early childhood education, we have observed over and again that many educators are stressed or confused, and some of our best practitioners have even left the profession – we commonly hear that 'The baby has been thrown out with the bath water!'. This has led to the success of our most popular professional learning session, 'Want your life back: effective and intentional planning and documentation', which we regularly present across the country.

This chapter aims to guide early childhood educators back to the basics of educating, back to the core business of the profession, and back to the basics of why and how to effectively plan and document. It will clarify the purpose of planning and documentation and then take you through the Walker Learning planning and documenting tools that provide everything that is needed for accountability and, more importantly, personalising learning for the children. In addition, we will share some ideas that have been big winners for many early childhood centres across the country. Of course, each educator needs to have the flexibility for their own style – but in this chapter we provide systems that you can adapt to your needs and the opportunity to provide continuity and consistency across all rooms, for educators, children and parents.

Back to basics and fundamentals

The Effective Provision of Pre-School Education Project (EPPE) is a significant and powerful study that has provided indisputable evidence about the importance and core elements of a high-quality early childhood education (Sylva et al. 2004). This study along with the Canadian Early Years Study (Akbari & McCuaig 2014) reminds us all that early childhood educators have one of the most important professions in the world. These studies reinforce that our profession is not 'babysitting' or 'playing all day'; whether with a baby or a five year old, we are teaching them, through play. We can teach, we can instruct, we can develop children through play. They also remind us that relationships are everything. It is disturbing to meet educators who appear not to have smiled at a child in years.

These studies remind us that relationships are critical and that teaching must be intentional. Chapters 2 and 4 provide more information on intentional teaching and building relationships. Successful and effective planning and documentation builds on these understandings and this practice. The first thing to address is the balance between time spent with children and time spent documenting. Ironically, despite all the evidence highlighting the importance of relationships with children, we find that early childhood educators are spending on average less than 20 per cent of their time in authentic time with the children and are spending nearly 80 per cent of their time documenting (Figure 7.1). This balance is completely at odds with early childhood education best practice – the time has come to reset the balance.

The first step in resetting this balance is to be really clear about our purpose when we document; that is, to examine our core purpose. The core purpose is to teach and for children to learn, in relationships and interactions through play, and to be intentional – not formal, but intentional. Often enthusiastic and passionate educators spend too much time writing things that are not relevant to the core purpose of early childhood education and/or taking hundreds of photos. We know some educators spend hours and hours writing 'learning stories' – that often in the end give very little information related to the key purpose of documenting children's skills or learning.

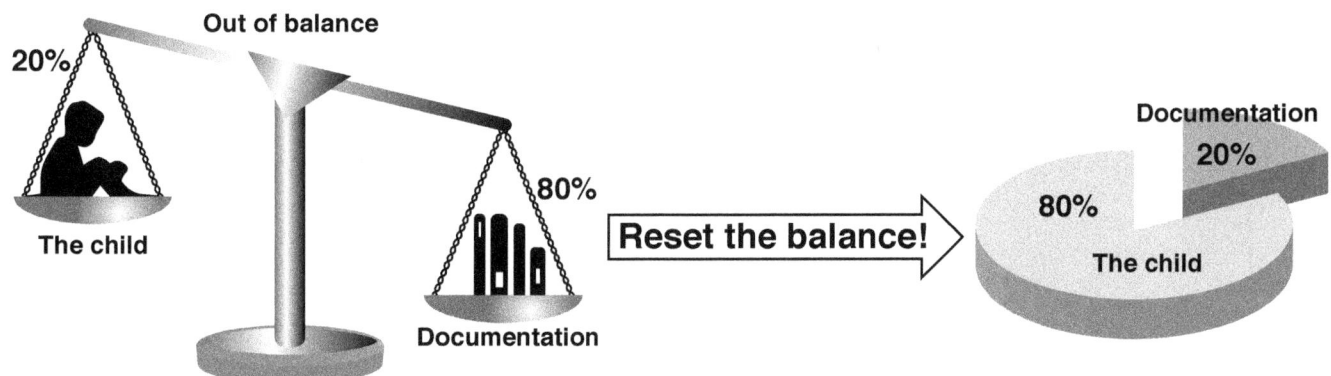

Figure 7.1 The first thing to address is the balance between time spent with children and time spent documenting. Ironically, despite all the evidence highlighting the importance of relationships with children, educators are spending, on average, less than 20% of their day in authentic time with children and nearly 80% of their day on documentation.

One aspect of documentation that may surprise many educators is that the key audience for documentation is ourselves, the educators! This has become lost and confused in recent years as many professional learning sessions and texts written about documentation have been heavily influenced by initiatives from overseas where time to document and cultural contexts are not relevant to the Australian context.

Key considerations and two key questions when we document require deep reflection at a professional and clinical level, and these are:

1. Why in fact do we document and for whom?
2. What information is necessary and how often?

The key purposes for documenting are to:

- ensure we know where a child was, where they are now and where they are headed so we can continue to scaffold, extend, intervene and support children in their learning, development and skill acquisition
- capture some of our intentions
- note some interests and something about the lives of the children in order to, at times, use these to further develop skills.

In other words, the educator needs to clearly document and articulate, 'What do I know now', 'What do I know about the child', and 'What am I going to do next' – this is why an educator documents.

Documentation in early childhood education is not (contrary to what has developed and spread like a virus across the entire country) to list, write narratives, stories and present art gallery standard pieces of work, photographs and art installations to impress adults, and which take hour upon hour to document and do not capture the learning, the skill or the development of the child.

We do not document by teaching to outcomes or cutting and pasting outcomes from the Framework. We do not teach to outcomes, but rather we teach children who deliver up hundreds upon hundreds of outcomes every week. The small list of outcomes listed in the Framework, which are a mix of values, learning outcomes, behaviours and a very small amount of development, run far too short on substance and distract educators from doing what they do best and have always done best, which is to *observe the child from what they see being demonstrated:*

- Is that child showing a left-hand preference?

- Is that child refining their tripod grip?
- Is that child reflecting self-regulation?
- Is that child pronouncing those sounds correctly?
- Is that child self-initiating?

These are the clinical, real and rigorous reporting outcomes that are scarcely written in any documentation and yet it is these very skills that need to be noted and identified, and in which some children may require early intervention, extension or scaffolding. It is these skills that parents are eager to read about and understand. And it is these skills plus early literacy and numeracy that have gone largely missing. Most early childhood educators wish desperately to bring rigorous and authentic documentation back and this book aims to liberate you to do just that.

You can bring back the rigour of skill and development into your records. Likewise, you can save time and effort by not buying into the myth that parents need to see everything every minute of every day, or that for effective communication with parents you need to write and photograph every detail of a child's life.

As highlighted in Chapters 1 and 2, early childhood educators do not teach to children's interests. That is what a good babysitter does. Documentation must document the learning and not patronise parents with pretty pictures about the sunny day and the blue sky. Our documents need to record the facts about development in family friendly but highly professional ways.

Rigorous documentation should be such that if another educator took over a program without a handover, they would know each child's learning and development through astute and simple records. Documentation that spends so much time on pages of notes that hardly anyone reads, and where educators are expected to take a certain number of photos each day and then cut and paste outcomes directly from the Framework, are missing the point, and educators are losing their independent professionalism. Educators need to write what they know from their expert body of knowledge about the developing child.

In summary, planning does not start with children's interests. Documentation is not about capturing moments. It is about the highly significant and important records of a highly educated clinician who knows all about child development, learning and skill and knows how to track this, understands that the primary purpose in education is for children to learn and develop, and that documentation needs to reflect that learning and development.

We don't help ourselves as a profession by spending time creating prettied-up pages with borders and motherhood statements about the child's 'lovely day' or a child having 'a sense of community'. We need to ensure that our documentation is user friendly, shared with parents but clinical, accessible and time saving. Early childhood education should not and does not need to prove itself to parents or others by having more documentation than any other sector of education.

Planning and documentation

Planning and documenting need not be a burden, stress or consume an educator's time at the expense of relationships with children and teaching.

We want educators to be in the moment with children, not busy documenting the moments with children.

Documentation is fundamentally, as in all major professions, about recording useful, accurate and up-to-date records of our clientele in order for us to know how to respond, plan and move (in our situation of education) children forward in their learning and development.

Remember the main audience for our documentation is ourselves!

We do wish to share our knowledge with families and have them share their knowledge and contexts with us. However, setting a healthy balance of what is necessary to know and how to share this is a very different professional dialogue than being driven by fear or inappropriate excessive expectations from parents or perceived expectations of government. Setting consistent and systemic planning that all educators across a centre use, ensures some key important fundamentals:

- It ensures consistency for all families as they may move from room to room over a number of years.
- It provides a high level of infrastructure systems to strengthen practices for all educators and a strong model which new staff can use once they commence.
- It reduces the worrying and at times destructive trend of comparison by parents and staff of how much or little a particular staff member has provided in way of documentation.
- It empowers all educators to concentrate on the rigour of recording skills, learning and development.
- It provides a greater body of professional records for other practitioners to access, who may be working with or assessing children, such as speech therapists, occupational therapists and general practitioners.
- It ensures parents are provided with a level of information that reflects their children's actual learning and development.

Establishing a system requires following and understanding a process of planning and recording. The key elements of planning and documenting include:

- process
- tools
- the nature and content of what is recorded.

Process

The process for planning and documentation operates through a feedback cycle (Figure 7.2), often referred to as a continuous improvement cycle. The starting point of this cycle, that informs all planning and documentation, is the educator's body of knowledge – the theories of play, developmentally appropriate practice, neuroscience and developmental psychology. The educator's body of knowledge is everything; it is what defines the early childhood education profession and must be the starting point for planning. The educator then develops and builds their knowledge of the child, the community context and the family. From this point the educator plans and implements through intentional teaching, the use of provocations, and scaffolding and modelling. The educator's body of knowledge is also the critical platform from which observations and assessments are made. Understanding this is essential – it should not be a process of copying and pasting outcomes from the Framework. Assessments are viewed as clinical, interpretive and analytical records of the child's learning, skills, development and understandings. They are the assessment of where the child is now and where to next for the child.

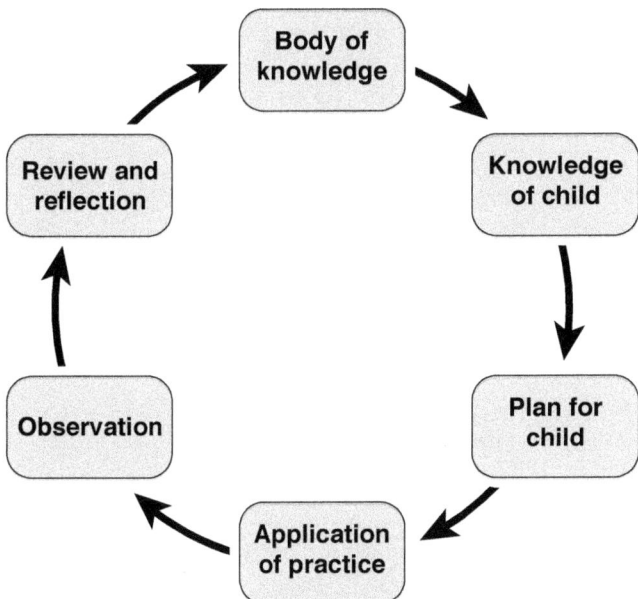

Figure 7.2 The process for planning and documentation operates through a feedback cycle, often referred to as a continuous improvement cycle.

This process also uses strength-based language and guides the educator to 'What next for the child', to build upon, to consolidate and to strengthen. This does not suggest that educators do not identify children's needs – as research has conclusively shown, the earlier the intervention and support the more likely the child will be okay. Once the feedback cycle has been completed, the educator uses this knowledge and reflects on it and reviews it relative to their body of knowledge, and the cycle then begins again. This cycle of continuous review, reflection on the child and the educator's body of knowledge is ongoing and takes place for each child on a regular basis.

Tools

A tool is simply a device we choose to use that help educators to document, collect and collate. It is important that the tools being used provide time-effective, authentic planning and documentation that personalises learning for every child while guiding the direction and learning for the whole group, communicating with parents and embracing the voice of the child. The following tools have been developed using international best practice in planning and documentation and have been successfully implemented in many early childhood education centres in Australia. The centres where we have worked and supported educators with their documentation and which have been through the National Quality Standard assessment process have all achieved the Exceeding level in this quality area using our documentation.

The following list of tools is what we call the imperatives. There are also tools, which are discussed later on in the chapter, which we call bonus or additional choices that individual centres may wish to use from time to time that may reflect their own values or philosophy, but are not to be confused with what we call the imperative tools which we discuss first. These are:

- daily/weekly record sheet
- individual observation and planning record (IOPR)
- daily reflection board/photos
- statement of intent (SOI)
- monthly evaluation by educators.

Each of the tools has a specific intention and when used together they provide effective and authentic planning and documentation.

In addition, educators would write a personal monthly critical reflection piece of perhaps half a page, and this is where the educators reflect on what they think has happened and what might need to happen. It might be on a learning area each month, or they might choose an area of the principles of practice ... 'I might work on my scaffolding', 'I might work on my open-ended areas', etc. This reflection is like a self-assessment.

Other ideas include:

- 'I might work on attention to detail in certain learning play areas.'
- 'I may extend my language skills in open-ended questions.'
- 'I may work on bonding with certain children in more depth.'

Daily/weekly record sheet

The Walker Learning daily/weekly record sheet is descriptive, not interpretive. This means that we are jotting down a few things onto a record sheet template that sits on a bench or in a cupboard (not one we carry around with us) and is used to describe (not interpret) what the child is doing.

The daily/weekly record sheet is for daily incidental scaffolding (Table 7.1) – at the end of each week there will be at least one entry for every child. At the beginning of the term, type the children's names into the template and make copies, one for each week of the term (each week the template is dated). These templates are filed at the end of each week, so there is a great record of patterns of play, and are then available and easily accessible to all educators working in the room. These records do not need to be rewritten or transcribed onto individual records of each child.

This tool is designed to literally document the educator's observations of where and what a child is engaged in during a session. Typical entries would document where a child is playing and with what, perhaps whom they play with, or their interests. For example, Kathy: in blocks, city skyscraper, or Shona: blocks, with Kathy, space rocket. Entries are very short (a few words) and take only a few seconds. All educators working in the room are encouraged to make entries (educators, coeducators, relievers).

It is not intended that observations be recorded for every child every day; there may be four or five entries per day. An observation would be made for each child a minimum of once per week. If at the end of the week a child has not had an observation recorded it is a prompt to connect with this child before the session ends.

Table 7.1 The Walker Learning daily/weekly record sheet is for daily incidental scaffolding – at the end of each week there will be at least one entry for every child. A shortened record sheet is shown here.

Walker Learning

Daily/weekly record sheet: Early Childhood Education				Date:	
Child	**Monday**	**Tuesday**	**Wednesday**	**Thursday**	**Friday**
Jacob	In small kinetic sand tray sifting the sand with Hussein			Camping in teepee outside with Hussein	
Hussein		Big outdoor blocks making train station			Cardboard box construction with Emily making big bridge
Mary		Climbing the tree with Elouera			
Kathy					Reading books under tree about horses
Noah	Using magnifying glass to look at hermit crab in science and nature		Using magnifying glass to look at snails outside		
Abdul		In vet clinic bandaging dog's leg			
Adam	Singing 'teddy bear teddy bear' and playing tambourine			Building house in sandpit with rubber tubing	
Thomas			With Kathy making big dog from boxes		
Emily			Cardboard box construction making a tower		
Elouera				Changing baby dolls' nappies	

This planner has three purposes. It:

1. provides prompts for daily scaffolding
2. ensures no child 'falls through the gaps'
3. chronologically records children's experiences during investigations.

1. Prompts for daily scaffolding

The first purpose of this tool is to add richness and intention to the environment on a daily basis. At the end of the session the educator scans the document – Kathy was building a high-rise, Shona was making pizzas in the home corner – and this gives an instant snapshot of some of the things that were happening during the session. This provides valuable information regarding provocations that can be included in the next session. It may be some pizza menus, or perhaps a few books on building. This helps to add in little daily provocations that are building on the children's interests. It also helps to meet the NQF requirements of everyone in the room contributing to the observations. So daily scaffolding is one intention of this tool: it extends, it scaffolds, it helps the educator to build upon what happened the day before. It helps with relationships – the educator knows what has been happening with the children.

2. Ensures no child 'falls through the gaps'

The second intention for this tool is that it is an audit. Are the educators capturing what is happening? Or are children slipping through the cracks? Are the children who always grab our attention the only ones whom we notice, or are we giving time to all of the children? It is a non-deficit approach and a strength-based approach – it ensures that no child falls through the 'cracks'. It enables educators to easily identify children that may have been missed during the week and need to be on an educator's radar in the coming session. This is reviewed and discussed by educators in the morning briefing; for example, 'Who will be mindful of Kathy today?'. This ensures that everyone is equal – everyone has a right.

3. Chronologically records children's experiences during investigations

The final purpose of the tool is that it is filed at the end of every week, so at the end of the year there is an enormous collection of information related to the children, their interests, their play and their habits. This tool provides an amazing record in descriptive form. Educators see the patterns of play, patterns of interest, and who they played with. Where do they tend to go? What choices do they make? It is a chronological history. It doesn't matter if anyone reads it – it is not an analysis, it is just a description, so there are no issues with confidentiality.

Individual observation and planning records (IOPR)

The individual observation and planning record (IOPR) is the key planning document for early childhood educators (Table 7.2). Each individual child has an IOPR. Educators use this document on a regular basis to capture skills, development and experiences/interests of each individual child, and to link to both development and learning. This document provides the system to personalise learning and document intention for every child – it provides the data to springboard into the 'what next' for each child. It is completed for each child three to four times each term (depending on the number of sessions per week, e.g. children attending full time or part time). Entries are interpretive/analytical and are no more than one to two sentences per area of development or learning (and require only three to five minutes to complete for each child). This document builds a rich and authentic chronological analytical–interpretive record for every child.

The importance of this document is that it is the major planning document for each individual child. This is where the educator's interpretation/analysis (not descriptive) of a child is recorded. In this document, the cells expand and each entry is dated. Every child has their own electronic record of their development and learning. As mentioned, educators would make entries in each child's IOPR perhaps three or four times a term; it is not necessary to make an entry in every cell each time the educator documents for the child. This captures the educator's key intentions and does not need to be every day or every week! This moves to the practice of documenting more meaningful information in a more time-effective way. It helps guide the educator to focus on the skills, the development and the understandings of the child. These data are a critical component of the planning cycle and documents where the child is now and what is next for the child. It is recommended that the centre has a systemised roster for IOPRs for children each week – documentation will of course be spontaneous as well – as this means that all children on the roster have entries in their IOPR and any other important data for other children.

Table 7.2 The Walker Learning individual observation and planning record (IOPR) is the key planning document for early childhood educators. Every child has their own electronic IOPR that documents skills, development and learning on a regular basis.

WalkerLearning

Individual observation and planning record (IOPR): Early Childhood Education

Child's name: Julie_____ Date of birth: _____

	DEVELOPMENT interpretation/intentions
Social	25/3 Julie engages predominantly solitary and picked up in parallel play. She has limited verbal interaction and eye contact with the other children.
	20/4 Julie engages in book reading with educator for 10 minutes alongside other children and can answer questions about a story.
Emotional	4/2 Julie was tearful on separation from parent, and needed educator support and reassurance.
	20/4 Julie now settles independently and is able to self-initiate and engage on most occasions.
Cognitive	4/2 Julie needed support with colour and shape matching to discern patterns. She demonstrated persistence to complete task.
Language	25/3 Julie chats readily with educators about her family.
	20/4 Julie is able to speak clearly and with accurate recall about recent events.
Physical	25/3 Julie painted at the easel using her RH, palmer grasp.
	20/4 Julie jumped both feet together. Successfully negotiated over the top of the A frame with appropriate hand placement.
Developmental intentions	Terms 1 & 2: To support Julie to engage in interactive/associative play.
	Develop fine motor strength and skill in the fingers.
	KEY LEARNING AREAS interpretation/intentions
Literacy observation	25/3 Julie regularly reads stories in reading area.
	20/4 Julie is identifying letters in her name and some text.
Literacy intention	Term 1: continue to look at picture story books with repetitive text.
Numeracy observation	25/3 Julie is recognising the shapes of leaves.
	20/4 Julie counted out pieces of fruit for her friends at morning tea up to 6.
Numeracy intention	Term 1: to extend Julie's understanding of 1:1 correspondence.
	KEY FRAMEWORK OUTCOMES interpretation/intentions
Community	25/3 Julie spends time in dramatic play, she enjoyed role-playing in the pizza restaurant.
Communication	4/2 Needs support with verbal expression of her emotions.
Identity	20/4 Julie has developed a confidence in the new environment and can independently settle and engage.
Well-being	20/4 Julie eagerly engages every session in creative art, outdoor play and music experiences.
Learning	25/3 Julie's visual spatial skills are developing, she now completes puzzles with more than 15 pieces.
	ADDITIONAL COMMENTS
Specific interests	Julie loves watching *Play School* and talking about Big Ted.
Additional information	Julie's father absent for 1 month due to work OS. This was unsettling for her.
Parent comments	Good to get feedback on Julie's missing Dad. We noticed it at home too.
Other comments	

NOTE: Educators may choose to use the National Early Years Framework outcomes in preference to the Developmental Domain Table. We strongly encourage educators to record these clinical observations from a developmental perspective.

The IOPR document has three major components. The first part is related to the child's development – educators can choose between working with the traditional developmental domains (emotional, social, cognitive, language, physical) and using the framework as a reference. Planning intention around elements of development has been missing in recent years, but it is an absolute necessity. Children are still developing and maturing. Development in the early years is something early childhood educators must be acutely aware of. In the first six years, early intervention is critical. If educators are not recording key aspects of a child's development and learning. They are not tracking with their professional expertise and knowledge the key aspects of the developing child that may require intervention or extension. Table 7.3 provides a brief description of each developmental domain; these are described in more detail in Chapter 1 and related to neuroscience in Chapter 3.

Table 7.3 Descriptions of developmental domains

Emotional
This is often also known as the affective domain. It refers to children's developing identity, self-concept, emotions, expression of needs and attachment. It encompasses the development of the self.
Social
This refers to the self in relation to others, and includes awareness of others, interactions, initiation of contact with others, relationships with others, pro-social skills, interpersonal communication and awareness of diversity.
Language
This refers mostly to oral and communicative language, language expression, verbal expression, speech, articulation, speaking, listening and vocabulary.
Cognitive
This refers to and means 'thinking skills'. Thinking includes problem solving, lateral and creative thought, perspective and sensorial awareness, decision making, imaginative thinking, initiative, prediction, memory and recall.
Physical
This refers to gross and fine motor skills, bilateral coordination, spatial awareness, body image and awareness and health.

The relationship between the National Early Years Framework (the Framework) and the development domains can be summarised as: community is mostly social; communication is mostly language; identity is mostly emotional; well-being is mostly physical; learning is mostly cognitive. If using the developmental domains, educators would use the Framework as an audit. It is not the case of educators simply copying and pasting the National Framework outcomes – as these outcomes are not all necessarily developmental outcomes, which not only leads to confusion, but also dilutes the rigour of the observations being recorded.

The second part of the IOPR document is related to literacy and numeracy intentions. The third part is for the parents to make contributions. This document is available for parents – and they love it! For families, the IOPR may be emailed once a term or as often as they or the educator wishes – this is just one way to communicate. Parents may or may not write back with contributions. It is also a very useful document to use in parent interviews, and this has been a big winner when talking to parents. It is highly professional, almost like a mid-year report. It can also be given to parents at the end of the year as a report, representing a whole year of skill and development. The IOPR is also a fabulous document to support transition reports.

Daily reflection board/photos

It is indeed sad to reflect that the majority of parents don't read or have time to read the written end-of-day daily reflection page. In addition, there is little point in sending an educator away from the children to write it up when no one reads it. It takes educators away from interacting with children, particularly when children most need extra time and attention from their educators.

At the end of the day, or at some time that suits children and educators, instead of writing a big reflection we suggest using a daily reflection board. The purpose of the daily reflection board is to document on a daily basis elements of the day that communicates something the children have (1) learned about today and (2) experienced today (Figure 7.3). If the children are old enough the educator could chat with the children, sometimes together as a group, a small group or individually scaffold the contribution of the children to this process – this also represents the child's voice. The scaffold may sound like, 'What is something we learned about today?', 'What are some of the experiences we had today?', 'What is something we enjoyed today?' This is about co-ownership, it's simple and gives 'agency' to the child and documents the child's voice. We try to avoid saying, 'What is something we *did* today?'

These reflections are written up on a whiteboard/blackboard/large paper with the day's date and the board or paper is positioned near the entrance of the room so parents can get a snapshot of the children's experiences and learning during the session. We recommend that these statements are documented – taking a photo of the board is easiest – here is your record of a daily reflection! This is filed for the educators' record but can also be emailed to parents at the end of the week along with a few reflection photos. This is particularly helpful for parents who may not come to collect their children or whose children travel by bus in remote areas and don't get to see these daily reflections.

These reflection boards are a wonderful opportunity for parents to begin conversations with their children about their day – it is great conversation starter for the family and the child and you. This facilitates the link and communication between home and centre.

Figure 7.3 The purpose of the daily reflection board is to document on a daily basis elements of the day that communicates something the children have (1) learned about today and (2) experienced today.

Statement of intent (SOI)

The final tool is the statement of intent (SOI), which is designed to guide the learning and experience of the room over the next few weeks (it informs parents and all educators of the intentions and experiences). It is not an old-fashioned planner, and it does not show the linking to everything with arrows, but rather it provides a guide of where everyone is heading in the next few weeks. The SOI is also flexible enough to be responsive to the children's particular needs, skills or interests as they arise. It is recommended that the SOI is completed electronically so that educators can copy and paste each fortnight into the next SOI for evaluation and planning. Table 7.4 provides an example of a completed SOI.

The SOI is a working document; educators and parents can contribute to it and it is reviewed on a fortnightly basis. The SOI provides a message to families, relievers and visitors that this is the centre's intention for the next few weeks. We don't start with a blank sheet and wait to see what happens. The purpose of the SOI is to indicate that we plan, we have intentions, and to show where we are heading, based on our daily/weekly record and our knowledge of individual children and our body of knowledge and expertise in early childhood education. This tool also builds and facilitates links between families and the centre.

The SOI is planned in columns working from left to right – this process ensures the educators move through the planning process in distinct stages. It starts with the child (development), then identifies the learning intentions (literacy and numeracy), the emergent curriculum (children's interests and parent contributions) and core curriculum (community experiences). When all this critical information has been documented the educator has internationally best practice data to use as an intentional guide to their environment, provocations and scaffolding and modelling.

Table 7.4 The Walker Learning statement of intent (SOI) is designed to provide for some of the learning and experience of the room over the next few weeks (it informs parents and all educators of some of the intentions and experiences planned). Spontaneous additional provocations and resources are added in response to children's experiences.

Walker Learning

Statement of intent: Early Childhood Education generic planning indicator (example for a 3 to 5 year old room)

Development	Learning/skill intentions	Children's current interests	Staff/centre/parent/ community interests	Snapshot of experiences and additional provocations	Reflection: other experiences as they emerge from children
Emotional For the children to: • separate from parents/carer • begin to feel secure in their new environment. **Social** For the children to: • grow in awareness of their peers • begin to respond to their educators. **Language** For the children to: • begin to learn the names of some of their peers and educators • begin to verbalise basic needs and wants (e.g. going to the toilet). **Cognitive** For the children to: • begin to explore a range of materials indoors and outdoors • begin to make choices of learning experiences. **Physical** For the children to: • become familiar with moving around the space both indoors and outdoors • have opportunities to build upon general gross motor coordination.	**Numeracy** For the children to: • understand that life has routine and predictability • experience natural shapes in the environment. **Literacy** For the children to: • be introduced to picture story books • be introduced to storytelling. **Science** For the children to: • explore how things move • explore and manipulate objects • experiment with different mediums.	• Fishing • Camping • Crocodiles • Beach • Dinosaurs • Football • Babies • Dogs • Dolls • Playground • ABC Kids • Trains	• Chinese New Year • Puppet show • Veggie patch • Circus in town • Fishing festival • Moomba festival **Parent contribution / comments** • Playing guitar • Cooking • We went camping • Got a new puppy • Grandparents arrive from overseas • Visited Puffing Billy • Dumpling making	**Dramatic play – camping site** • Books • Fishing rod • Baby bed in the tent **Sensory** • Sand with crocodiles • Books on crocodiles and reptiles • Clay with icy pole sticks, gum nuts, leaves, seedpods **Construction** • Blocks • Books on playgrounds • Train tracks • Books on trains **Collage** • Bark and rocks that you might find in a campsite **Reading** • Chinese New Year • Book of families at centre • Camping • Photos of families • Puppies **Literacy resource** • Desk (home style) • Letter paper • Envelopes • Keyboard **Tinkering** • Wheels/cogs • Nuts and bolts • Chains, locks and keys **Science and nature** • Shells/stones/sponges/sand • Fishing reel • Tank with sea creatures **Chinese New Year** A few artefacts around the environment	• Sally made a city skyscraper next to the trains • Sally got out some books on city buildings • Jarrod wanted to set up a pig shooters licence on the campsite • Billy dressed up as a Chinese dragon • Children made a lake in sandpit for the crocodiles

Early Childhood Play Matters

The following text examines in more detail each stage of this planning process.

Stage 1: Development domains

This is the starting point where the educator documents some elements of the foci on child development – as an example – for the children to practise making a decision, or for children to strengthen fine motor skills in the fingers. The setting of the developmental domain intentions is the first and most critical part of the planning process. It is what essentially makes the difference between this approach and other approaches to curriculum design and planning. Deficit models are not used in our planning. Rather, the approach seeks to identify both needs and strengths of each child to build upon, extend or intervene in – this is a non-deficit model. The developmental domain intentions are highly specific so that measurement can be undertaken during the educator's observations. They will also be the basis for the ways in which many of the actual learning experiences are set up.

The wording that frames this part of the documentation is: 'For the children to …' (e.g. for the children to work in parallel alongside each other). This helps the educator to explicitly highlight what it is they want for the children's learning. For example, for the children to:

- be introduced to
- consolidate
- demonstrate
- revise
- extend.

Note that when using the SOI, as shown in Table 7.4, educators may choose to develop their intentions from the National Early Years Framework outcomes in preference to the Developmental Domain Table. We strongly encourage educators to record these intentions from a developmental perspective.

Stage 2: Learning intentions

This is where the intentions are related to literacy and numeracy (e.g. for the educators to model language of size and colour).

These areas of literacy and numeracy are very rarely displayed or planned or highlighted in early childhood education and they need to be.

These concepts of course are modelled all of the time, but are listed from time to time on the SOI to remind staff and parents that learning and modelling of skills and concepts are continually being scaffolded in areas of learning such as literacy and numeracy, and that parents can model and reinforce these concepts at home in everyday play events. For example, in the learning intention column under numeracy we might write 'For the children to be introduced to terms such as under, over, through and across'. This might be demonstrated by educators when children are moving through an obstacle course or building with the outdoor blocks.

Early childhood education is always modelling literacy and numeracy, and educators must not fall into the trap of thinking that because we use play-based, non-formal instruction we are not actively scaffolding broad-based literacy and numeracy skills (e.g. communicating, self-expression – through multiple mediums – dramatising, storytelling, singing, role play, mathematical concepts).

Stage 3: Emergent curriculum identifying children's interests

This is where the educator documents the children's authentic interests – what they enjoy doing when they are not at the centre, or what is a particular interest in this stage of their lives.

Stage 4: Core curriculum identifying community centre experiences

This is where the educator brings current community activities or experiences to the children's learning experiences. Little children don't know what they don't know and this is where the educator exposes children to new and different experiences – it's about what is happening in the wider world, our community, festivals, seasons, events … These experiences are not themes or topics, but things that are happening, things we want to expose the children to. For example, some children we have worked with have been refugees who have lived in detention for most of their life, and they have never been to the beach. In this column the educator may list 'the beach', not because it's a topic or a theme or a project, but because it is a new experience!

Community interests are added in as intentions at this stage. For example, the language used is not, 'We are doing sustainability', but rather, considering the stage of development and understanding of children in the early years, the intention might read, 'For the children to take responsibility for recycling their materials, lunch scraps and litter'. Specifying community interests with an intention before the actual focus or content helps to ensure that the learning is developmentally appropriate and not just about values of a particular community. Remember that due to the egocentric nature of children's brain maturity, attempting to get them to appreciate or understand the worldwide implications of sustainability is inappropriate. Starting with the immediate world of young children is more meaningful and relevant to their own lives. Starting with an intention also helps the educator to focus on the skill or understanding to be developed.

This way of thinking also helps to build inclusive approaches to community events and to children and families of culturally diverse backgrounds, with a range of family structures, and with a range of interests and needs. Instead of thinking about 'doing a project on family', the intentions might include, 'To promote thinking about people who are important in our lives', to help children identify people significant to them. One of the ways of meeting this intention may be to discuss family types, but there is also a wider range of strategies and ideas that can be used in order to meet these intentions. This broadens the scope of the discussion and helps to engage children who will also identify their own interpretations and experiences.

The other key element of this stage is parent contributions; it invites parents to document activities and experiences the families are being involved in. Parents might document 'I can come in and make spring rolls' or 'I play the guitar'. Educators brainstorm the range of interests that the children currently display. These are used as ideas for some of the provocations and experiences that will be promoted during the next fortnight for further learning.

Stage 5: Identifying learning experiences, provocations, scaffolding and modelling

This is finally where the educator plans the actual learning experiences – in a child-centred pedagogy the educator can only plan the learning experiences once they have the knowledge and understanding gained through the completion of the prior four stages. In traditional teaching, the planning often starts at Stage 5 ('What are we doing?') rather than at Stage 1 ('What do we want for the children?'). Once the educator has completed columns 1 to 4 this is all they need to extend and develop their rich and intentional learning environment, to identify and add provocations (related to any aspect of columns 1 to 4). This stage also guides educators about the scaffolding and modelling that has been intentionally documented. For example, if we know that a child is now using words related to measurement, such as long, high, short, and we also know they love constructing in the block area, we can plan to scaffold through the blocks by placing objects to measure with, informal and formal tools of measurement, such as rulers, tape measures, string and wool.

Stage 5 involves planning for the children during the following fortnight. The planning includes all aspects of the day and week and the actual experiences should attempt to include developmental and learning intentions. Setting up a range of activities (dramatic play, blocks and constructions) and provocations which reflect the interests of the children provides many opportunities for them to experience some of the intentions the educator may have set. It is important to note that it is not necessary or practical to provide different and individual experiences for every child in the group. Personalising the work and learning is based on the nature of and range of experiences that allow individual children to explore in many ways that are meaningful to them, rather than having separate work for each child.

Stage 6: The adult role

This part of the plan helps to focus the educator on what specific areas or major strategies they will be working on. It may include specific language, ideas to model or instruction strategies that will be a prompt for the educator. It can also be useful for parent helpers, additional educators and relief educators in understanding some of the goals for learning. It is the role of the educator, being intentional, purposeful and actively engaged with the child that brings play-based curriculum into a true teaching and learning approach. The educator's role must be part of the planning process.

Stage 7: Modifications and additions

Walker Learning is a responsive pedagogy framed by learning and developmental teaching intentions, thus the teaching must be flexible and dynamic. The modifications and additions provide this flexibility and dynamism by adding, deleting, changing and modifying some of the experiences and to capture some of these on the planning document. The planning has been developed to be dynamic, responsive and open to change.

These documenting tools are all you need (assuming that the content is of good quality!) and meet the requirements for an Exceeding level for the NQF. The good news is that these tools will reset the balance of teaching so that 80 per cent of your time will be with the children and only 20 per cent of your time will be spent on documentation.

The nature and content of what is recorded

When educators are documenting observations it is important to focus on being explicit and concise and to minimise flowery descriptive content (e.g. no 'fluff'). Extensive flowery descriptive content not only wastes an educator's time, but it dilutes and masks the important components of documentation (clinical-analytical analysis).

Documentation should:

- relate to an individual's skills, learning and interests
- be intentional
- include opportunities for parent inclusivity
- be culturally appropriate
- be available to share with parents
- be regularly updated.

The 'what' of documentation is:

- skills and processes related to learning
- conceptual understandings
- specific interests
- what next for the child
- parent information
- child contribution.

Other tools, templates and processes

The reader may have noticed that we have not mentioned portfolios or learning stories. It's not that you cannot use them, but they are not necessary and certainly not mandatory. The Walker Learning planning and assessment documents cover all the requirements – it is this simple. Any additional planning and documentation that an educator chooses to use is considered a bonus.

Portfolios

Portfolios are often time-consuming and in many instances become overwhelming for educators. If educators document using the above tools, portfolios will not be a necessary document. Educators and centres might want to compile portfolios, but this is a choice and not a mandatory or essential component of documenting. Portfolios are often just for parents and families – we know that these are highly valued by families. They love the memento. It is lovely. So you might decide that you want to go above the line of what is required and produce portfolios. Perhaps you can give families a gift at the end of the year that has a few photos. The best portfolio is a memento! It's authentic and it's real. And it should not waste your time as you work out what outcome it links back to, or create page borders, or make a publishable document. The first step in making the decision about a portfolio is to remember that a portfolio is a memento (it is not for the government) and to be clear on its purpose. If you choose to use a portfolio as a memento, you can do whatever you want. It is your personal choice. We recommend that you put in some photos, some special pieces, and you might let the children choose some of them.

You might have a paper version or a digital version – with face recognition software. There is no need to do this every day – if you are using the other documents.

So you might have a working portfolio throughout the year where the children might choose, or you might just do it yourself. Whatever you choose, you must have an agreement across the centre, so that you do not cause confusion and create a problems with the car-park chatter (that often occurs as parents come and go)! The portfolio must be unified – how many pages will it have? You need an agreement at the beginning of the year on what it will look like and what it will not look like. It also needs to be fair – you must have an agreement and the standard must be the same across all staff. This is not about personal choice, because as professionals working under the same roof, you must present a united front. You can be professional and make information available for families without having to spend your weekends organising photos and writing.

Learning story hysteria

Learning stories have morphed into a 'monster' for many early childhood educators in Australia. Learning stories originated from New Zealand where educators were given significant time to write the stories and they were not pages in length. As with portfolios, learning stories are not mandatory and are something an educator or centre would do from a position of choice, rather than from a position of compulsion. If there is a choice to write a learning story, we recommend keeping it brief. Educators might choose occasionally to write up a story on the photo board, or to write a few comments with revolving photos. Make it simple! Another option would be to choose one of the clinical notes documented in the IOPR, link it to a photo and then develop a short descriptive paragraph (maximum two paragraphs) to frame the experience. Then at the bottom of the paragraph the learning experience can be linked to the Framework.

Clipboard and camera intrusion

- The time has come for educations to regulate the use of the camera – have a whole week off from looking at children through a lens.

- We value relationships over recording, communication rather than records.

- Children are getting used to performing – take a photo of me! We need a balance here – children need you, not the camera. You as an educator and the centre have to set the boundaries and decide what is enough to know – it is the early childhood educators that set the standard (not the parents).

- Similarly, avoid walking around the centre with a clipboard, head down documenting and missing the child. We have even heard an educator say 'Can you say that again while I write it down', and witnessed one educator not actually educating because their role was to take notes.

- Using the Walker Learning tools will not require educators to be consumed by their clipboards and cameras – the Walker Learning Tools will liberate them to being authentic early childhood educators.

Summary

The key aims of this chapter are to show that:

- we want educators to be in the moment with children, not busy documenting the moments of children
- documentation and planning requires a clinical eye and professional, succinct records that provide opportunities for educators and parents to map and track the development, learning and interests of children
- using a system of documents that are consistent across a centre ensures a consistent message for children and parents; it provides a professional body of information sharing for educators across and between groups, and raises the standard of documentation for all staff
- capturing key skills, and learning and focusing on these rather than documenting interests, ensures that we are educating children, not merely capturing interests and not just babysitting.

Suggested resources

DVDs, books and online modules available at Early Life Foundations: http://www.earlylife.com.au

Chapter 8

Walker Learning: early childhood education (babies to preschool)

'Not all children are ready to learn the same thing at the same time in the same way.'

Kathy Walker

Introduction

Walker Learning (WL) is an Australian-designed teaching and learning approach (pedagogy) that engages children in active learning and is culturally and developmentally appropriate across all demographic regions of the country from remote Indigenous communities to elite independent centres and schools. Walker Learning authentically personalises learning and provides learning that is real, relevant and meaningful for all children regardless of their age, culture, family context, socioeconomic background or geographical position. Walker Learning has been developed in the Australian setting over 20 years using an action research model.

Walker Learning acknowledges that culture, community and family have a significant impact on a child's life and learning. However, it would be naive to ignore the importance of the biology on the developing child, just as it would be naive to ignore the importance of culture on the developing child. Walker Learning's evidence based on neuroscience and development. This evidence-based approach brings rigour, facts and the tracking and observation of children's development, learning and skill acquisition back to being the major role and focus in early childhood education.

In addition, a major aim of early childhood education is to ensure effective and smooth transition for children as they move between their early childhood and early primary years. Walker Learning ensures a consistency of teaching and learning across the early childhood and primary years. It provides systems for planning, documentation, implementation and relationships, and defines open-ended play-based curriculum based on child development theories.

To summarise the key principles of Walker Learning that we have outlined throughout *Early Childhood Play Matters*:

- Walker Learning is a play- and personalised-based pedagogy implemented across Australia and internationally for over 20 years.
- Walker Learning has been developed to embrace play pedagogy not only in early childhood but into the first three years of school and then extended into project-based learning across Years 3 to 8. With other great educational philosophies, such as Montessori, Reggio Emilia Approach and Steiner, Walker Learning is defined by a clear educational philosophy and theory.
- Walker Learning brings to early childhood an Australian-designed culturally appropriate play-based pedagogy that has been developed for the diverse range of Australian communities. It is the first time Australia has had an Australian-designed play-based curriculum.
- Walker Learning embraces the concept of the 'whole child'. We embrace the child holistically in terms of their overall development, using neuroscience and developmental theory as a foundation. We embrace culture and family and relationships within and beyond community as major influences in a child's life and learning.
- Walker Learning accepts the diversity of children, families and cultures and recognises that all children are born with the natural ability to learn and develop by exploration, investigation and the need for explicit direction and instruction. The whole child concept includes the child as capable and an active participant in their learning alongside the adult and extended community.

This chapter outlines how all of the key elements that we have discussed in this text look in practice throughout a day or week. In particular we highlight:

- the emphasis upon relationships (rather than an over-emphasis upon documentation)
- the use of evidence about the brain and development alongside culture, community and family for planning
- that our starting point is our knowledge base and *not* the children's interests (even though of course we include them)
- that we set up the learning environment with rich provocations, rich print and attention to detail
- Walker Learning provides open ended-experiences
- cosy corners that define small areas for children

- print, text and books are included in most learning play areas
- an emphasis is placed upon the personal and professional growth of educators in self-awareness and self-management in a deep way of mindfulness
- intrinsic rather than extrinsic motivation is used for learning and behaviour strategies.

This chapter also describes the terminology used in Walker Learning so there is greater consistency across all educators, families and children; this provides greater security and predictability in the children's lives. It describes how:

- sessions begin
- we explicitly build relationships
- we model language and communication skills
- we can build upon daily provocations without carrying notepads and clipboards around with us during the session.

The chapter starts with a description of the core elements that frame Walker Learning from early childhood to Year 8. Building on this platform we present the additional unique aspects of Walker Learning that are used in early childhood. The chapter concludes with how a typical Walker Learning day would look in babies, toddlers and three-year-old rooms and the preschool (four to five year olds).

Walker Learning: key elements (early childhood to Year 8)

The uniqueness of Walker Learning is that it provides a consistency of key elements, appropriate for the specific age and development of children, their learning requirements and skills as they move between their early childhood and primary years, thus allowing for a smooth and consistent teaching and learning approach as children make the transition between one year and the next (Table 8.1).

Table 8.1 The key principles that guide Walker Learning key practices across all stages of development

Key principles guiding Walker Learning key practices
• All teaching is intentional – either proactive or responsive.
• Not all children are ready to learn the same thing at the same time in the same way.
• Skills, learning and development are the heart of play and personalised learning.
• Children's interests are incorporated into learning at times, not for the interest alone, but as one way for engaging the learning and teaching skills.
• Children's interest, culture and context are respected and used as a springboard to facilitate further understandings and skill development in all areas of learning, including literacy, numeracy, the sciences, the arts, language, cognition, social, psychological and emotional development.
• Child development, neuroscience and developmental psychology are the main elements used as a basis for guiding practices as well as the principles of culture, community and family.
• The process of learning and skill acquisition is valued – not the focus on the end product.
• Intrinsic (not extrinsic) motivation is valued and embedded in practice.
• The adult/child relationship is highly valued and the relationship itself is a scaffold in the learning alongside the child.
• Relationships with child, family and community are integral components of the approach.
• Walker Learning does not require topics or themes, but does include specific concepts from all subject disciplines.
• Relationships are developed and deepened through a range of key practices including focus children.

Walker Learning is an entire approach and philosophy, not simply one pedagogical tool or system. This means that rather than just adding one particular additional tool into the day, the approach is holistic and impacts on everything within the learning environment. Similar language, terms and key aspects of the approach, how it is implemented and the role of the educator are reflected in the approach whether children are toddlers or in Year 6. Obviously how the teaching looks will change as children move through the year levels and according to curriculum demands. The Walker Learning philosophy is based upon the belief that consistency in language, learning environments, planning and strategies assist children, educators and parents as they move from their early childhood and throughout their primary years. This text sets the foundation upon which Walker Learning moves into the early primary years (Foundation to Year 2 – Play matters) and then our project-based approach in Years 3 to 8 (Engagement matters).

Walker Learning embraces and embeds:
- the use of peer as the model
- the use of children's interests and the environment for engagement
- scaffolding and modeling by the educator.

Walker Learning: key pedagogical practice across early childhood to Year 8

There are key elements of Walker Learning that are considered 'not negotiable' and hold the approach together in terms of maintaining the rigour of the pedagogy. There are additional developmentally appropriate elements that are incorporated into the pedagogy and are unique to each stage of development: early childhood, Foundation to Year 2, and Years 3 to 8. This provides continuity and consistency as a child moves from preschool into the early, middle and upper years of primary school alongside elements that are uniquely suited to the child's stage of development. Below is a list of the core elements of Walker Learning from preschool to Year 8, and in the subsequent section the unique components additional to early childhood are introduced.

Table 8.2 This table captures the unique key elements that define Walker Learning from preschool to Year 8

Unique elements of Walker Learning Practice preschool to Year 8		
Preschool to Year 2	**Year 3 to 8**	**Planning and documentation (preschool to Year 8)**
• Focus children	• Focus children	• Statement of intent (SOI)
• Tuning in and reflection	• Tuning in and reflection	• Individual observation planning record (IOPR)
• Learning environment	• Learning environment	• Daily/weekly record sheet*
• Investigations	• Education research project (ERP)	• Daily reflection board*
• Children's interests	• Children's interest	* Documents for preschool to Year 2
• Reporter and photographer	• Expo	
• Freebies	• Communication board	
• Parent information board	• Clinic groups	
	• Class meeting	

NOTE: In addition to the unique elements of Walker Learning the explicit teaching of numeracy and literacy and other curriculum areas and all requirements of National Curriculum Frameworks are included.

Focus children

Relationships with children is the cornerstone of Walker Learning. As discussed in Chapter 4, relationships are critical to a child's learning, and an educator who develops resonance with the child through an empathy response enhances a child's confidence to take risks in their learning, helps the child to transition through difficult times at home, and is able to pitch learning at just the right level for that child. The primary purpose of focus children is relationship development – this is the opportunity for the educator to spend special time (a few minutes) with the focus child a couple of times over the course of the day or the session. There will be a focus child roster where each child will be a focus child once every two to three weeks; this is dependent on the size of the class and in the early childhood setting dependent on the number of sessions per week. The focus child system is based on a non-deficit model where no matter who the child is, and no matter what their challenges or strengths are, the child (and parents) and the educator know they will be the focus on average once every two weeks.

Children love being the focus child and often have trouble waiting their turn (a great opportunity for them to practise self-regulation!). When asked 'What does it mean to be the focus child?', a Year 1 boy responded with a huge smile on his face 'It means I am on my teachers radar!'.

The educator will differentiate how they work with the focus children in response to the child's stage of development – clearly working with a five year old will look very different to working with a 10 year old. Despite this, the key purpose and role of the focus children is the same across all levels and is as follows:

- The primary purpose of a focus child is to build relationships between educator and child.
- Focus children stand at the front of the group for a few minutes during tuning in. The educator scaffolds and discusses in front of the group something the focus child is interested in and for the educator to scaffold this interest related to their learning. The scaffolding doesn't need to link to current learning intentions, simply to whatever skills, learning or development that the opportunity presents. In early childhood this may be scaffolding 1:1 or 1: small group or as the year progresses 1: whole group.
- The educator honours the authentic interests of the focus child and uses these interests as the platform to scaffold and model the learning.
- During investigations, focus children spend a few minutes each on their own with the educator. This ensures relationship building, personalised scaffolding and time for the educator to get to know more about the child.
- Focus children report back at reflection time on their learning. Children ask questions and the educator scaffolds specific examples of learning, skills, behaviour and values. In early childhood this may be scaffolding 1:1 or 1: small group or as the year progresses 1: whole group.

Tuning in and reflection

Tuning in represents *tuning in for the learning for the whole day* and involves 20 minutes of scaffolding and modelling from the educator in front of all the children (sitting on the mat) and using the peer as the model. Successful tuning in requires the educator to be intentional and responsive, using sophisticated scaffolding skills and working from the learning intentions in the statement of intent (see Chapter 7).

In early childhood, tuning in will be a combination of scaffolding 1:1 or 1: small group, or as the year progresses 1: whole group. If the educator is using 1: whole group, the tuning in would be a shorter time (about 10 minutes). In Years 3 to 8 tuning in will take place any time in the morning and may be in a 20-minute block or smaller units of time adding up to 20 minutes.

The key components of tuning in across all levels are:

- welcome and administration
- reflection and revision of learning intentions
- focus children scaffolding in front of the group.

Reflection time is where the focus children have the opportunity to reflect on their learning and for the educator to scaffold the learning that has taken place during investigations (or in Years 3 to 8 the learning that has taken place across the day). In Foundation to Year 2 reflection is used as a 'springboard' into formal teaching; in the early childhood years, reflection is the opportunity for the educator to scaffold the learning that has taken place in a way that is real, relevant and meaningful to the children. This includes:

- scaffolding focus children
- the educator modelling particular skills and concepts from investigations or across the day in Years 3 to 8.

Tuning in and reflection are powerful models of teaching based on the neuroscience evidence described in Chapter 3. These include:

- repeat, repeat and repeat – tuning in and reflection provide the opportunity for children's learning to be presented repeatedly in small 'chunks' in a scaffolded conversation. A skilled educator can revisit learning, concepts and understandings in a real and relevant way multiple times during tuning in and reflection
- scaffolding learning through children's interests provides contextual learning opportunities
- the educator is the first teacher, the child is the second teacher and the environment is the 'third teacher' (making connections through children's investigations and provocations; see also Chapter 6).

Investigations (play-based learning)/education research projects

Walker Learning is a play-based pedagogy in early childhood and the early years of primary school. In early childhood, investigations are based on exploratory play which takes place throughout the day (or session) with the educator scaffolding and modelling the learning in 1:1 or 1:small groups. There is no formal teaching of literacy or numeracy in early childhood. How this looks in early childhood settings is described below.

In the early years of primary school, at least four mornings each week, the day will start with active, hands-on experiences for the children known as *investigations*. Each day there will be formal instruction in numeracy, literacy and specialist subjects. The experiences of the children and the explicit teaching that takes place during investigations are used as a springboard into the formal teaching of the day.

In Years 3 to 8 the education research project replaces investigation time and involves formal teacher-directed learning (immersion) alongside student-directed project work.

Children's interests

Walker Learning uses children's interests as one part of the learning cycle. The beginning of planning and the establishment of play-based learning is not children's interests, but due to the open-ended nature of investigations, both indoors and outdoors, children are free to explore, create and express their own interests or creativity in any way they wish.

Learning environment

Walker Learning views the learning environment as the 'third teacher' and setting up an engaging and intentional learning environment takes great care and expertise. The environment set-up is informed by child development theory, the intentional planning of the educator and the current interests of the children and the school community. Setting up the environment appropriately is one of the keys to engaging the children. Chapter 6 provides specific instruction on setting up an exploratory play-based environment for early childhood settings. The key requirements are:

- preferably both indoor and outdoor settings
- at least 12 different learning play areas that are play-based and open-ended
- print-rich experiences or resources within some of the key learning play areas
- well-organised, clearly defined spaces that are divided up into sections (little rooms within the room).

Notice board: parent/communication

A notice board is an important conduit for communication to the parents in the early childhood and early primary years. In Years 3 to 8 the notice board is used as a communication board for the children and the educator – it is a dynamic board that develops independence and ownership of the child's learning.

The key elements of the notice board across all levels are the:

- focus child roster
- statement of intent
- key learning intentions.

Planning and documentation

Planning and documentation holds the implementation of Walker Learning together and ensures rigour; it also provides the insurance for educators to know they are assessing and documenting with clarity and purpose. It ensures that all our provocations, scaffolding, extension and intervention, our relationships with children and our tuning in and reflection are intentional and responsive to children. The two planning and documenting templates that are used across all levels are the statement of intent (SOI) and the individual observation and planning record (IOPR). In the early childhood years there is also the daily/weekly record and the daily reflection board (described briefly below). Each template has specific purposes and each complements the other so that when they are used together no additional templates are needed. Walker Learning planning always clearly articulates, 'What is it that we want the children to learn?', and always includes developmental intentions along with literacy, numeracy and other subject intentions. The planning and documentation used in early childhood is briefly described below and presented in far more detail, including the purpose of each document and how it is used, in Chapter 7.

Walker Learning: key pedagogical practice in early childhood

In addition to the key elements presented above there are several additional elements unique to early childhood and the early years of primary school. These are described to the right.

Reporter and photographer

The reporter and photographer are educator-directed roles. The educator introduces the task and requirements of the reporter and photographer at tuning in each morning. At reflection time, the reporter and photographer report back and share whatever their task was.

The educator sets the reporter's task. In this way, each child has a personalised task set for them. The reporter role is a favourite role as each child feels special and has a task that scaffolds their learning without being too difficult or demanding. The reporter only has to carry out the role for part of the investigation time and then they can proceed back to their own investigation.

In early childhood, a photographer may be used before introducing a reporter. This is at the educator's discretion and highly personalised so that each child is provided with a task that is pitched just right for his or her needs and learning. The task would take less than 10 minutes to complete and should be exciting and fun. Early in the year, the photographer's role could be as simple as photographing the focus children or finding as many different shapes as possible around the classroom. Other examples of a photographer's role could include:

- taking some photos of children working outside
- taking five photos today.

The reporter's role is similar to the photographer's. The task is set by the educator and may involve a broad range of skills and tasks. The task would take less than 10 minutes to complete and should be exciting and fun. Examples of a reporter's role could include:

- drawing something outside
- collecting a basket of different shaped leaves or pebbles from outside.

Each day the photographer's and reporter's role will be different. It should not be a case of regurgitating the same tasks each day. The idea is that each day the role is different and personalised for the child who is taking on this role.

Intentional dispersal

Intentional dispersal refers to the process the educator uses to scaffold the children to begin investigations at the end of tuning in. This is an important component of the child's development and executive function – making decisions, maintaining focus, self-initiating and engaging. The aim of intentional dispersal is that no child leaves the mat without intent. The general flow of intentional dispersal is:

- focus children, reporter and photographer go to investigations
- educator disperses other children once intention has been identified for each child
- dispersal may be in small groups or individually
- some children will require additional help to develop intention, self-initiation and then engagement – the educator keeps these children until last so they can scaffold these children as needed.

In early childhood, many children may still require time to look around, or may still be at the onlooker play or solitary play stage. They may not yet know where or what they wish to engage with. The intentional dispersal is really to assist children with learning how to think, to imagine, to plan or to experience choice making.

Freebies

'Freebies' are a wonderful opportunity for educators and the children. Each day there will be one or two freebies that the educator will use during reflection to intentionally scaffold the children's learning. There are three broad categories of freebies:

1. Intentional teaching: one or two children who used a provocation during investigation and who did something that can be used to demonstrate or model or practice a development, literacy or numeracy skill that is being focused on at the current time.

2. Responsive teaching: a child who did something during investigation that was too good to miss, even though it may not have been related to the current learning intentions.

3. Affirming a child who has had a challenging time (for any reason) and in this session they have had a 'moment of goodness' or relative success. The educator uses this freebie as an opportunity to really affirm a child who is needy.

Resetting the environment

Involving the children in resetting the environment provides them with is an important and powerful learning opportunity. Be mindful that not all children have to reset the environment every day; some children may be tired or unwell and may just need a rest. The key components of resetting are to:

- help children take responsibility for their learning
- plan ahead and think about what resources or books they may need for the next day
- promote continuity and persistence
- set up the 'work in progress' signs and shelf
- allow time to take additional photos that may be needed
- pack away slowly, carefully, thoughtfully and methodically, not rushing around madly.

Planning and documenting

Planning and documentation is covered extensively in Chapter 7. Here we provide a brief overview of the documents used in early childhood.

Individual observation and planning record (IOPR)

- This is the major planning document for early childhood educators.
- Educators use this document on a regular basis to capture skills, development and experiences/interests of the individual child and to link to both development and learning.
- This document provides the system to personalise learning and document intention for every child – it provides the data to springboard into the 'what next' for each child.
- It is completed for each child three to four times each term (depending on whether they

are full or part time). Entries are clinical/analytical and are no more than one to two sentences per area of development or learning (and require only three to five minutes to complete for each child).

Statement of intent (SOI)

- The SOI provides a snapshot of where the educators are heading over a two- to three-week period based on the individual records of each child and encourages parent input and contributions.
- It identifies some general foci and is displayed for parents with the intention to build links between home and the centre.

Daily/weekly record sheet

This is for daily incidental scaffolding – at the end of each week there will be at least one entry for every child. It literally documents the educator's observations (not interpretive or clinical). This planner has three purposes. It:

1. provides prompts for provocations
2. ensures no child 'falls through the gaps'
3. is a chronological record of children's experiences during investigations/exploratory play.

Daily reflection board

The purpose of the daily reflection board is to document on a daily basis elements that communicate something the children have (1) learned about today and (2) experienced today. If the children are old enough the educator would chat with the children, sometimes together as a group, small group or individually and scaffold the contribution of the children to this process – this also represents the child's voice. The scaffold may sound like, 'What is something we learned about today?', 'What are some of the experiences we had today?', 'What is something we enjoyed today?'. It's about the co-ownership, it's simple and gives 'agency' to the child and documents the child's voice. We try to avoid saying, 'What is something we *did* today?'

Implementation of Walker Learning: babies to preschool

Walker Learning philosophy guides the evidence-based practice that is implemented from babies through to Year 8. As described above there are core elements that are 'not negotiable' from preschool to Year 8 with additional elements that are threaded into the pedagogy to suit the developmental stage of the children. Due to the unique needs of children in the early years not all of these core elements are included. In this section we examine Walker Learning implementation for babies through to preschoolers. This section builds on the knowledge presented so far in this text. In particular we refer the reader to the chapters on neuroscience (Chapter 4) and setting up the learning environment (Chapter 6).

Walker Learning for babies and toddlers

Walker Learning has some key principles of practice for this age group. These include:

- the rooms should not look like mini versions of the preschool rooms
- minimal tables and chairs
- lots of rugs, sofas, different surfaces to crawl and walk on
- small cubby type places
- access to outdoors with real grass, trees, dirt, sand
- opportunities for the babies and toddlers to play alone
- relationships are paramount
- primary carer for each baby and toddler
- ideally, the same group moves from the babies' room the following year with the same educators into the toddlers room to maximise relationships and attachment, and so all children and educators remain together for at least two years

- babies and toddlers are not moved into another year level during the year to prevent disrupting attachment and established relationships
- the concept of the 'focus child' is introduced at a beginner level.

Walker Learning for three year olds

Walker Learning for three year olds includes focus children, the photographer's role for some children who may be ready for this role, and occasionally, particularly during the latter part of a year, the reporter.

Formal times of tuning in and reflection are usually short five- to ten-minute chats that may include songs and stories, and settle children into the day. They may be conducted upon arrival or after the children have settled into their play and all children have arrived.

Walker Learning for four to five year olds

There are a number of options for this age group. Sometimes upon arrival the children just start straight into investigations and then once they have all arrived, the educator will bring them back to start a tuning in. During Term 1 this is shorter than a normal tuning in and less formal (usually about five to ten minutes).

General intentions and experiences are discussed along with the options the children have to choose from during the session. This may involve an indoor and outdoor choice, or one or the other depending on the individual centre. There may or may not be a photographer or reporter early in Term 1 but it depends upon the group and prior experiences. After dispersal and investigating inside and outside there would be a reflection just before lunchtime. In between there may be a story or song or game in a short group time that is invitational. Not all children are expected to attend the group time and may continue to engage in their play if they wish. There is no need to have lots of tuning in and reflection times each time they are grouped.

After lunch, the educator might have a semi tuning in again without the focus children to reset their intentions and highlight any new provocations that have been put out. Another reflection of the day is at the end and this may include some songs or games. Table 8.2 shows a typical daily schedule.

Table 8.2 Example of a typical daily schedule for a whole day session for preschool children

Time	Schedule
8:00 a.m.	Arrive and welcome
8:30	Tuning in
8:45	Outside–inside investigation
9:45	Reset outside–inside
10:00	Tune in – revisit
	Inside investigation
11:10	Reflection time
	Reset playroom
11:30	Lunch time
12:15 p.m.	Outside investigation
1:00	Reset outside
1:15	Rest
1:30	Investigation inside
2:00	Reflection time
	Reset playroom
2:30	Singing, movement and dance
2:45	Pack bags
	Home time

Summary

The uniqueness of Walker Learning is that it provides a consistency of core elements, appropriate for the specific age and development of children, their learning requirements and skills as they move between their early childhood and primary years. There are additional developmentally appropriate elements that are incorporated into the pedagogy and are unique to each stage of development: early childhood, Foundation to Year 2, and Years 3 to 8. This provides continuity and consistency as a child moves from preschool into the early, middle and upper years of primary school, alongside elements that are uniquely suited to the child's stage of development. There are core elements of Walker Learning that are considered 'not negotiable' and hold the approach together in terms of maintaining the rigour of the pedagogy.

Implementing the core elements of Walker Learning are critical for the success of the pedagogy; however, the approach offers great fluidity and flexibility of practice in the early childhood years. This flexibility accommodates the range of diversity within each community around Australia and internationally. Walker Learning provides educators with the opportunity to use initiative and discretion to be intentional, responsive and spontaneous with individuals and groups.

Built into this flexibility are the foundational elements that define Walker Learning as a pedagogy that personalises learning and is developmentally and culturally appropriate. These key principles are considered 'not negotiable' and include: focus children, relationship and attachment, open-ended learning play areas, defined and small learning centres, rich print and text, attention to detail in all provocations, the full range of learning play areas, the value of indoor and outdoor learning, the use of natural and authentic materials and resources, and the non-use of technology as an activity.

The intention of Walker Learning in the early childhood years is:

- to ensure that relationships are a key focus
- that the outdoor learning area is considered to be as equal to indoor space, and is understood as being extremely important in learning for children. The use of outdoor space provides connectedness and continuity with the indoor experiences along with being an area in its own right. As with the indoor environment, the outdoor environment is developed with intention (related to development, learning and children's interests), and experiences are open-ended with intentional provocations
- to set up as small spaces, cosy corners, nooks and crannies for individuals or small numbers (two to three children) rather than tables of four to six
- systems of tuning in, reflecting, focus children, reporters and photographers, are embedded
- to provide continuity and consistency for all educators, children and families
- that primary carers and attachment are assured for babies and toddlers by implementing a two-year cycle of educators and children remaining together.

Suggested resources

DVD: *Walker Learning model teaching Foundation to Year 2.*

DVD: *Walker Learning setting up an intentional and engaging learning environment.*

DVDs, books and online modules available at http://www.earlylife.com.au

Bibliography

Akbari, E & McCuaig, K 2014, *Early Childhood Education Report 2014,* Ontario Institute for Studies in Education, Toronto. Available at http://www.earlyyearsstudy.ca.

Bass, S & Walker, K (DVD), *Setting up and engaging and intentional learning environment.*

Berk, L & Winsler, A 1995, 'Vygotsky: his life and works' and 'Vygotsky's approach to development', in *Scaffolding children's learning: Vygotsky and early childhood learning,* National Association for Education of Young Children, Washington, DC.

Center on the Developing Child 2011, *Building the brain's 'air traffic control' system: how early experiences shape the development of executive function,* Working paper 11, Harvard University, Cambridge, MA.

Chess, S, & Thomas, A 1984, *Origins and evolution of behavior disorders,* Harvard University Press, Cambridge, MA.

Copple, C & Bredekamp, S (eds) 2009, *Developmentally appropriate practice in early childhood programs: serving children from birth through age 8,* National Association for the Education of Young Children, Washington, DC.

Coyle, D 2010, *The talent code. Greatness isn't born it's grown,* Arrow Books, London.

Department of Education, Employment and Workplace Relations 2009, *Belonging, being & becoming. The Early Years Learning Framework for Australia.* Available at https://www.coag.gov.au/sites/default/files/early_years_learning_framework.pdf

Elkind, D 2007, *The power of play: learning what comes naturally,* DeCapo Press, Philadelphia.

Epstein, AS 2007, *The intentional teacher: choosing the best strategies for young children's learning,* National Association for the Education of Young Children, Washington, DC.

Feldman, J & Mulle, K 2007, *Put emotional intelligence to work,* American Society of Training and Development, Alexandria, VA.

Golinkoff, RM, Hirsh-Pasek, K & Eyer, D 2004, *Einstein never used flashcards: how our children really learn – and why they need to play more and memorize less,* Rodale Books, New York.

Kelly-Byrne, D 1989, *A child's play life: an ethnographic study,* Teachers College Press, New York.

Lengua, LJ, Honorado, E & Bush, NR 2007, 'Contextual risk and parenting as predictors of effortful control and social competence in preschool children', *Journal of Applied Developmental Psychology,* 28(1), 40–55.

Lindsey, G 1998, 'Brain research and implications for early childhood education', *Childhood Education,* 75(2), 97–100.

Liston, C, McEwen, B & Casey, B 2009, 'Psychosocial stress reversibly disrupts prefrontal processing and attentional control', *Proceedings of the National Academy of Sciences,* 106(3), 912–17.

Liston, C, Miller, M, Goldwater, D, Radley, J, Rocher, A, Morrison, P & McEwen, B 2006, 'Stress induced alterations in prefrontal cortical dendritic morphology predict selective impairments in perceptual attentional set-shifting', *The Journal of Neuroscience,* 26(30), 7870–4.

Manne, A 2014, *The life of I. The new culture of narcissism,* Melbourne University Press, Carlton, Victoria.

Marcon, R 2003, 'Reply to Lonigan commentary', *Early Childhood Research and Practice,* 5(1), http://ecrp.uiuc.edu/v5n1/marcon.html.

Marotz, LR & Allen, KE 2013, *Developmental profiles: pre-birth through adolescence,* 7th edn, Wadsworth, Belmont, CA.

Maughan, A & Cicchetti, D 2002, 'Impact of child maltreatment and interadult violence on children's emotion regulation abilities and socioemotional adjustment', *Child Development*, 73(5), 1525–42.

Medina, J 2012, *Brain rules: 12 principles for surviving and thriving at work, home and school*, Scribe, Brunswick, Victoria.

Medina, J 2014, *Brain rules for baby. How to raise a smart and happy child from zero to five*, Scribe, Brunswick, Victoria.

Melhuish, E 2015, 'Early childhood environments: long-term consequences of early childhood education and parenting', in S Hay (ed.), *Early years education and care*, Routledge, Oxford.

Melhuish, E, Belsky, J, Leyland, AH & Barnes, J 2008, 'Effects of fully-established Sure Start Local Programmes on 3-year-old children and their families living in England: a quasi-experimental observational study', *The Lancet*, 372(9650), 1641–7.

Neven, RS 1996, *Emotional milestones from birth to adulthood: a psychodynamic approach (Annals of Child Development)* Paperback, January, Cambridge, MA.

O'Connor, TG, Rutter, M, Beckett, C, Keaveney, L & Kreppner, JM 2000, 'The effects of global severe privation on cognitive competence: extension and longitudinal follow-up', *Child Development*, 71(2), 376–90.

OECD 2015, 'Skills for social progress: the power of social and emotional skills', in OECD Skills Studies series (ed.), OECD, Paris.

Schweinhart, LJ & Weikart, DP 1997, *Lasting differences: the HighScope Preschool Curriculum Comparison study through age 23 (Monographs of the HighScope Educational Research Foundation, 12)*, HighScope Press, Ypsilanti, MI.

Stacey, S 2009, *Emergent curriculum in early childhood settings: from theory to practice*, Redleaf Press, St Paul, Minnesota.

Sylva, K, Melhuish, E, Sammons, P, Siraj-Blatchford, I & Taggart, B 2004, *The Effective Provision of Pre-School Education (EPPE) Project: final report. A longitudinal study funded by the DfES 1997–2004*, Institute of Education, University of London.

The Third Teacher, http://www.thethirdteacher.com.

Thomas, A & Chess, S 1977, *Temperament and development*, Brunner/Mazel, Oxford, England.

Vygotsky, L 1978, 'Interaction between learning and development' (pp. 79–91), in *Mind in society* (trans. M Cole), Harvard University Press, Cambridge, MA.

Wood, E & Attfield, J 2005, *Play, learning and the early childhood curriculum*, 2nd edn, Paul Chapman Publishing, London.

Index

Note: *Bold italic* indicates figures/tables
CS indicates colour section

assessment, 76–90
attachment, 32–3, ***33***; building, 44–5

babies and toddlers, 68–9, *see CS*
babies to preschool, Walker Learning implementation, 101–2
Bass-Walker Systems Model, ***7***
behaviour, 43–4; proactive strategy guidance for, 44–8
best practice, alignment with DAP, 8
brain development, 25; uniqueness and diversity, 30

cameras, 90
child-initiated play, 57
children, ***45***; children's interests, 20–1, 57, 87, 98; communication, relationships, and working proactively with, 38–50; educators–children intentional relationships, 17; falling through 'gaps,' 82; focus children, 97; guiding, 43–4; knowing, 42–3; ownership of play, 57; thinking processes through play, 58; whole-child concept, ***7***
clipboards, 90
closed activities, 72–3
cognitive domain, 9–10, 84
cognitive flexibility, 26
collage, 64, 66, *see CS*
colleagues, communication, relationships, and working proactively with, 38–50
communication: with children, colleagues and parents, 38–50; notice boards, 98–9; proactive communication strategies, 46–8
community centre experiences, 87–8
conflict, 50
construction, 64, 66–7, *see CS*
constructive and investigative play, 55
contextual experiences, 31–2

daily reflection boards, 84–5, ***85***, 101
daily/weekly record sheet 80–2, ***81***
deep learning paradox, 30
deep structural learning, 32
development: developmental domains, 8–10, ***84***, 87; related factors, 10–11, ***11***
developmentally appropriate practice (DAP), 7–12; alignment with best practice, 8
documentation *see* planning and documentation
dramatic play, 31, 64, 65, *see CS*
dynamism, 89

early childhood education, 2–12; back to basics, 76–8; information technology in, 73; intentional teaching development, 17–20; personalised learning informed by child development, 8; Walker Learning, 94–102
early childhood pedagogy, 34
early childhood to Year 8: Walker Learning key – pedagogical practice, 96–101; key elements, 95–6
education research projects, 98
educational philosophy development, 2–7
emotional (or affective) domain, 9, 84
emotional intelligence (EI) and model, 38–44, ***40***, 50; assumptions, 39

emotional regulation, 39
empathy, 34, 39
engagement, 48–9; engaging learning environment, key features of, 69–73; learning environment's invitation to engage, 71
equity, 24–5
evidence-based practice, ***6***, 24–34
executive function skills, 25–8, ***26***, ***27***

flexibility, 89
freebies, 100

genotype, 24–5
group time area, 71–2

'I' messages, 46–7
imaginative and socio-dramatic play, 55
individual observation and planning records (IOPR), 82–4, ***83***
information technology, 73
inhibitory control, 26
intention, 16–17, 20–1; learning intentions, 87; proactive and responsive, 19–20; for process not project, 20
intentional dispersal, 100
intentional teaching, 16–21; informed by child development, 8
interactions, 18–19
investigations, 82, 97, 98

language domain, 10, 84
learning environment – engaging and intentional, 18, 62–73, 88, 98; attention to detail, 70; defining learning experiences and spaces, 69–70; design elements, 70–1; key features, 69–73; key learning play areas, ***63–4***; resetting, 100; resources and materials, 71
learning experiences: contextual experience and repetition, 31–2; defining, 69–70; key learning experiences, 62–9
learning stories, 90
literacy: literary resource, 64, 67, *see CS*; resources for linking play to, 72

modelling, 34, 84, 88

National Early Years Framework (the Framework), 2, 5, 17
National Quality Framework (NQF), 64, 89–90
nature and nurture, 24–5
neuroscience, 24–34; developmental neuroscience, early childhood pedagogy implications, 34; neural plasticity, 25
non-verbal communication, 33
numeracy: numeracy resource, 64, 67, *see CS*; resources for linking play to, 72

open-ended play experiences, 30–1, 31; *versus* closed activities, 72–3
oral language, 58
Organisation for Economic Cooperation and Development (OECD) report, 28–9
outdoor learning, 68, *see CS*

painting and drawing, 64, 67–8, *see CS*
parents, communication, relationships, and working proactively with, 38–50
pedagogical practice, 96–101
pedagogy, 31, 34, 54–5, 96–101
persistence, 73

personal inclination, 4–5, ***6***
philosophy (of centres), 49
physical domain, 10, 84
planning and documentation, ***77***, 78–90, ***79***, 99, 100–1; intentional planning, 18; planning element provocations, ***63***; process, 79, ***79***; tools, 80
play: active, purposeful and creative nature, 57; involves literacy and numeracy, 57–8; key characteristics, 57–8; learning–teaching–play links, 58; as process, not just end product, 57; social skills and oral language promotion, 58; stages – explorative, sensory, onlooker, parallel, associative, cooperative, 56; teaching–learning perspective, 54–8; types of, 55
play-based pedagogy, 54–5
portfolios, 2, 89–90
proactive prepared intention, 19–20
proactivity, 44–8; *versus* reactivity, 44; working proactively, 49–50
provocations, 18, 31–2, 62, ***63***, 88

reading, 64, 66, *see CS*
record sheets, 80–2, ***81***, ***83***
reflection, 84–5, 97–8; reflective listening, 46
registered training authorities (RTAs), 2
relationships, 32–3; building, 38–48, 44–5; with children, colleagues and parents, 38–50; educators–children intentional relationships, 17; face time, 32–4; relationship management, 43–4
repetition, 31–2
reporter and photographer, 99

scaffolding, 16–17, 18–19, 26–7, 31, 57, ***81***, 82, 88
science and nature, 64, 67, *see CS*
self-knowledge and self-management, 40–2
sensory play, 31, 64, 65–6, *see CS*
social and emotional skills, 28–9, ***29***
social awareness and understanding, 42–3
social domain, 9, 84
social skills, 58
statement of intent (SOI), 85–9, ***86***
strategies, 49; proactive strategies, 44–8
stressful situations, 27–8
symbolic play, 57

temperament – goodness of fit, 47–8
tinkering and carpentry, 64, 67, *see CS*
trust, building, 44–5
tuning in, 97–8

verbal communication, 33

Walker Learning, 8, 42, 55, 94–102; for babies and toddlers, 101–2; developmental practice examples, 11–12; for four to five year olds, 102; implementation, 101–2; individual observation and planning records (IOPR), 82–4, ***83***; key elements, 95–6, ***96***; key pedagogical practice, ***95***, 96–101; play stages and, 56; record sheets, 80–2, ***81***; for three year olds, 102
working memory, 26

'zone of proximal development,' 30

www.ingramcontent.com/pod-product-compliance
Lightning Source LLC
Chambersburg PA
CBHW061127070526
44584CB00033B/4241